MARCO POLO

CRETE

BULGARIA

Black Sea

MK (F.Y.R.O.M.)

ALBA-NIA

Thessaloniki

Athens

TURKEY

GREECE

Iráklio

Crete

CYPRUS

Mediterranean Sea

LIBYA

EGYPT

www.ma

D0234343

THE TOURING APP

shows you the way...
including routes and offline maps!

FREE!

GET MORE OUT OF YOUR MARCO POLO GUIDE

IT'S AS SIMPLE AS THIS

1 go.marco-polo.com/cre

2 download and discover

GO!

WORKS OFFLINE!

SYMBOLS

INSIDER TIP	Insider Tip
★	Highlight
●●●●	Best of ...
☆	Scenic view
♻	Responsible travel: for ecological or fair trade aspects
(*)	Telephone numbers that are not toll-free

PRICE CATEGORIES HOTELS

Expensive	over 120 euros
Moderate	70–120 euros
Budget	under 70 euros

Prices for a double room in peak season, with breakfast in a hotel, without breakfast in a guesthouse or studio

PRICE CATEGORIES RESTAURANTS

Expensive	over 18 euros
Moderate	13–18 euros
Budget	under 13 euros

Prices for a main course with side dishes and salad. Fish can be expensive

CONTENTS

MAPS IN THE GUIDEBOOK
(142 A1) Page numbers
and coordinates refer to
the road atlas
Coordinates are also given for
places that are not marked
on the road atlas

(🛍 A–B 2–3) refers to the
removable pull-out map

INSIDE FRONT COVER:
The best highlights

INSIDE BACK COVER:
Maps of Chaniá, Réthimno,
Ágios Nikólaos, Iráklio

The best MARCO POLO Insider Tips

Our top 15 Insider Tips

INSIDER TIP ▸ Wet or dry?

The Wets enjoy the finest cocktails at *Wets & Drys*. The Drys stay outside because you need a code to enter. But it's shared with anyone. Which is why the 'in' scene of Iráklio meets here on the dot of 7.20pm – who cares about the prohibition → p. 64

INSIDER TIP ▸ A real farmer's market

Every Saturday the lively farming village of Míres has a large *farmer's market* (photo above), well away from the tourist bustle → p. 70

INSIDER TIP ▸ Family-friendly gorge

Wandering through the *Iríni Gorge* is easy – even with young children – and it is usually open even when the famous Samariá Gorge (photo right) is closed due to rockfall hazards. When you reach the end you can take a public bus or taxi back to the starting point → p. 42

INSIDER TIP ▸ E-bikes with Adam

E-bikes are for sissies? You'll change your mind after a tour of the mountains with *Adam Frogákis*! → p. 120

INSIDER TIP ▸ Georgína's clutches

The post-modern clutch bags in coloured leather by designer Georgína Skalídi could be haute couture – were it not for the (affordable) prices → p. 36

INSIDER TIP ▸ Avocado beauty

In the peaceful mountain village of Argiroúpoli Cretan avocados are processed into *cosmetics* and coffee and cocoa powder substitutes are produced from locally grown carob tree pods → p. 53

INSIDER TIP ▸ A priest with a passion for collecting

In Asómatos, Pápa Michális has his own *village museum* and his daughter-in-law Sísi knows the history of every object → p. 54

INSIDER TIP Lonely isle
Koufonísi has long been uninhabited. The old Roman theatre is sinking in the sand while the turquoise waves lap gently agains the white sandy beaches. You can get here from Makrígialos → p. 88

INSIDER TIP Wellness in the harbour
Al Hammam is an oriental wellness temple in the harbour of Chaniá where you can chill like the Sultan would have, with views of the tavernas and the sea → p. 121

INSIDER TIP Up, up and away
Kapetanianá in the *Asterússia Mountains* is the new hotspot for climbers in the Mediterranean. You can also learn it here → p. 118

INSIDER TIP Traveller's nest
The *Cretan Villa* was originally used as Ierápetra's hospital but today it is one of the most popular meeting places on the island. Manólis, the friendly landlord, treats his guests as though they are family → p. 87

INSIDER TIP Fata Morgana
In the stony landscape of Káto Zákros, *Stella's Apartments* seem like a mirage – blue and white houses in a lush garden → p. 99

INSIDER TIP Guaranteed adrenaline rush
In Arádena on the south coast the brave can do a 138 m/453 ft *bungee jump* → p. 118

INSIDER TIP Please call!
The landlady of the small bed and breakfast *Archontikó* in Sitía only takes reservations by phone. This way, she gets friendly guests – and they can really relax and enjoy their stay there → p. 95

INSIDER TIP Digitalised hotel
Olive Green is the new hotel in which digital natives are able to handle almost everything using an iPod, tablet or smartphone. The central location is wonderfully convenient, while the eco-friendly interior is good for the conscience → p. 64

BEST OF ...

FOR FREE

● *A night on the beach*
Your beach mat as a mattress, a pareo to cover you – and you're ready for a midsummer night on the beach. Best of all on *Gávdos*, Europe's southernmost island. It's something lots of people do here, and the police have better things to do than to disturb the sleepers – because they're asleep too → **p. 40**

● *Ride your own roller coaster*
Think Crete is fabulous, but you're missing the roller coasters? Then enjoy the ride from the north coast to Chóra Sfakíon. The *serpentine road* from the Askífou Plateau down to the Libyan Sea is as good as any fun park → **p. 40**

● *Free concerts*
Admission to all the concerts held at the four-day *Houdétsi Festival* of Cretan music is free for visitors – the sponsors pay all the costs → **p. 127**

● *Where the olive oil flows*
The young proprietor of the *Paráskákis* olive oil factory will show you the secrets of harvesting olive oil and you can also go on a free guided tour of the ultra modern facility in Melidóni → **p. 56**

● *Free admission to the pool*
Admission prices into waterparks are usually extremely expensive but you can enter the *Star Beach Water Park* in Limenas Chersónisou for free. You only pay to ride the slides → **p. 124**

● *Górtis: ruins in an olive grove*
After seeing the Odéon and Títus Basilica of Górtis, many travel further and miss out on a lovely walk through the ruins of the Roman city, which lie between age-old olive groves and – totally unlike the excavations on the opposite side of the road – they are also free of charge (photo) → **p. 70**

ONLY ON CRETE
Unique experiences

● The sound of lyres in Chaniá
The *lýra* and *laouto* are Crete's traditional musical instruments. Every night you can hear them being played in the modern Ouzerí *Chalkína* in Chaniá's old town, for local and foreign guests. The lyrics are mostly about love and the fight for freedom → p. 37

● Vámos: live in the town
If you rent one of the restored houses in *Vámos* you will be in the centre of the town's day-to-day life, enjoy regional specialities in some of Crete's best tavernas and discover Crete's nature during walks → p. 45

● Rakí and mezédes
When *mezédes* (photo) are served your table will be laden with a variety of small dishes. As an accompaniment to the tasty morsels Cretans love to drink *rakí* from small decanters. The ideal venue for this is called *rakádika* and a number of them are squeezed into the Odós Vernárdou in Réthimno. → p. 50

● Back to the hippies
Mátala became famous in the Sixties, when hippes came from all over the world to live here. Every year around Whitsun, the spirit of Woodstock is rekindled during the *Matala Beach Festival*. The stage is set up on the beach, and there's a campsite right behind it. With the celebrated Caves of Matala before their eyes, the music unites all generations, and once again the motto is: 3 days of music and peace → p. 126

● Surrounded by mountains
Uninhabited plateaus are a geographic characteristic of the island. During the summer countless sheep and goats graze here and during the winter they are covered in snow. The *Nída Plateau* just under the summit of mount Psilorítis is easy to reach and beautiful to stroll through → p. 65

● Nightlife in Iráklio
In the street cafés surrounding the *Platía Korái* in the heart of Iráklio, mostly young Cretans sit on trendy lounge furniture, meet their friends and listen to music. The popular drink from early morning until late at night is iced coffee in many varieties → p. 63

ONLY ON

BEST OF ...

AND IF IT RAINS?
Activities to brighten your day

● *Marine life*
When it is raining visit Greece's most modern aquarium. There are over 2500 creatures in the *Cretaquarium* (photo) in Goúrnes, among them octopus, lobsters, seahorses and sharks → p. 124

● *Just dive in*
Rainy days are ideal for scuba diving – children can learn using special equipment in the hotel pool and adults in the open sea – use an outfit like the *Atlantis Diving Centre* near Réthimno → p. 120

● *Scary rather than pretty*
Some experiences are best had by pretending rather than having them for real. One such experience is an *earthquake simulator*. The *Natural History Museum* in Iráklio offers it every 30 minutes. Nice to be so safe while you're having it → p. 61

● *Descend into the underworld of Zonianá*
Descend 550 m/1800 ft into the underworld of stalagmites and stalactites in the *Sventóni stalactite cave* – and discover the beautiful forms created by water → p. 68

● *Pottery village*
Margarítes is home to studios of more than 20 potters, so close together that it doesn't even matter if rains. There's often a delightful symbiosis of the artistic and the useful – and the items don't cost the earth → p. 55

● *Lovely to touch*
If you can overcome your fear, you'll instantly know how lovely snakes actually feel. You can stroke the pythons at *Reptisland* in Melidóni. They are guaranteed not to be hungry → p. 55

RAIN

RELAX AND CHILL OUT
Take it easy and spoil yourself

● *Feel the earth's forces at Ágios Pávlos*

Between Ágios Pávlos and Préveli on the south coast, you can feel the exceptional forces of the earth. Because of this several providers offer workshops for yoga, meditation and t'ai chi here → **p. 121**

● *Back to nature*

In *Miliá*, rock replaces the walls of some houses. In 13 restored natural stone houses, candles are used at night, drinking water is carried from a nearby fountain and the village taverna takes care of your well-being with produce and fresh ingredients from the region (photo). You will not hear a single car, nothing disturbs your self-concentration → **p. 43**

● *Easy into the night*

Music for chilling and relaxing to is played in Chaniá at the *Fagotto*, the island's oldest jazz pub. The cocktails are just as good as the old town ambience → **p. 37**

● *Comfortable train trip*

Have you ever had a ride in a *trenáki*? This mini train with three carriages trundles on rubber wheels across many Cretan country roads. You sit in open mini-carriages, feel the wind through your hair and arrive at your destination completely stress-free. The excursion programme is especially extensive in Georgioúpoli → **p. 124**

● *Relax with Hollywood stars*

Get yourself a drink at the bar and enjoy an evening in an outdoor cinema. The best is the summer cinema *Astéria* in Réthimno's old town where Hollywood movies are shown directly in front of the Venetian fortress walls → **p. 50**

● *In the town park*

Mocha served in a brass pot, oriental cakes. The menu even has Champagne. PlayTávli – or Monopoly, if you prefer. The *O Kípos* coffee house in the town park is a haven of peace, and not just for the locals. And the summer cinema is right next door → **p. 35**

INTRODUCTION

DISCOVER CRETE!

Wow – done it! The road winds up the steep slope like the thread of a corkscrew. A few houses are scattered down below, in the glowing sun on the *coastal plain*. On the edge of the steppe-like landscape, the old fort of Frangokastéllo broods over a wide sandy beach. Beyond that, the sea doesn't reach land again until Libya. There is a *touch of Africa* in the air – and occasionally a little dust from the Sahara blows over to this, the southern coast.

A *rustic kafenió* dozes in the sun at the entrance to the first mountain village you come to. Landlady Janina is Danish, and speaks many languages. Her Creton husband Bábis has decorated the airy terrace with horned goat skulls. The mountain tea is freshly brewed, and a lavender stalk floats on top of the carob lemonade. Classic music plays gently in the background, and the *home-pressed wine* tastes of the Creton soil. It's easy to forget the rest of the world here in Kallikrátis – but that's not to say the Cretons are behind the times. You can expect to have free *wi-fi access* in even the tiniest mountain village and every pub. And most kafeníos have the TV on virtually around the clock, although using it is different. Perhaps like in the large mountain village of Anógia.

Crete's interior with mountain villages and beautiful monasteries is as diverse as the coast

It is still early in the year. In the modest Kafenío at the platía, the *coffee shop on the town square*, wood is crackling in the fireplace. Chairs with woven seats line three of the walls, turned towards the centre. Against the fourth wall, behind the counter, the host brews *rich coffee* in brass and copper pots, pours it into small espresso cups and serves it to the guests with a glass of water.

> **Mocha in a brass pot? You'll find it here**

Just above the counter is a huge *flat screen television – made in Japan –* broadcasting an important soccer match. Everyone is watching and commentating. Then the half-time whistle. A guest turns off the television. Two young men, both in Cretan

INTRODUCTION

OFI Iráklio shirts, grab their *lýras*, an age-old Cretan instrument, and begin playing and singing masterfully. Crete becomes tangible through all the senses. After 15 minutes, the television is turned on again, the music dies down. An American fast-food chain advertises their hamburgers, and then the soccer players continue their game.

Time hasn't stood still on Crete, either. Gigantic **wind turbines** rotate on mountain ridges, and on the motorways and dual carriageways of the north coast, the Cretans rush from town to town while quads drone down the alleyways of Mália, rather popular with young British people, a few miles from the *Aegean coast* there are now water parks with loud music and giant water-slides. For holidaymakers who prefer being taken care of there are a number of all-inclusive hotels and holiday resorts and one luxury hotel in Eloúnda even offers *helicopter transfers and butler services* with the holiday villa that also comes with a private pool. In Iráklio an EU institute takes care of the data security of the whole of Europe, while on the south coast Chinese in-

Crete is part of the globalised world

vestors want to build a large container ship harbour for the distribution of their wares in the Mediterranean and Black Seas. On the *Lassíthi Plateau*, Albanian migrant workers harvest organically grown potatoes and the Pakistani shepherds can phone home to their hearts' content from the back of their donkey or the seat of their moped because of a *flat rate*. Crete is now very much a part of the globalised world and wants to keep it that way.

But Crete also has another interesting and distinctive side. Travelling from the airport, one cannot help but notice the *bullet holes* in the street signs. They serve as target practice for many Cretans. Every shot is an expression of the locals' unease over *too much state authority*. The small mountain village of Zonianá made headlines when citizens protested against a large police presence after a narcotics investigation – according to them the sight of all the uniforms would have a negative impact on the children. This situation must have felt like an echo from their past under *foreign rule*: until Crete's union with Greece in 1912 and during the German occupation (1941–44) every act of resistance against the state authorities was seen as an act of bravery and is still praised in school text books. To this day the Cretan motto remains: „Freedom or death!"

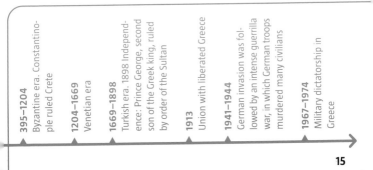

395–1204 Byzantine era. Constantinople ruled Crete

1204–1669 Venetian era

1669–1898 Turkish era. 1898 Independence: Prince George, second son of the Greek king, ruled by order of the Sultan

1913 Union with liberated Greece

1941–1944 German invasion was followed by an intense guerrilla war, in which German troops murdered many civilians

1967–1974 Military dictatorship in Greece

Despite this behaviour Crete remains one of the safest holiday destinations in the world. For centuries, *hospitality* has been one of their top priorities and as a tourist you will always experience it – certainly when you are away from the tourist centres. *Rakí* and fruit are served as dessert free of charge in most tavernas where the owner also often invites the guests to a cup of Greek coffee. And if you should stumble on a *village wedding*, you may well be invited to stay and join in with the celebrations.

Some 623,000 people live on the island, over 200,000 of them in the greater area of the *capital Iráklio*. The other major island towns are all situated on the north coast. But there is no need for visitors to get stressed. Although the island's history is omnipotent in many of the old buildings, it is integrated almost casually into modern life. The order of the day is: no rushing through; just enjoy yourself. *Chaniá*, which is still surrounded by medieval walls on the land side, can be explored either by horse-drawn carriage or Segway. The park-like castle of *Réthimno* has a summer theatre where plays and concerts of all kinds of music are performed. In fact, music is even played in what used to be a mosque. Against the bleached façades of old houses in the *Venetian harbour* of Réthimno, you can enjoy the freshest fish as it is prepared directly from the fishing boats. And in the Venetian shipyard in the harbour of Chaniá, the *Freddo espresso with views of the Aegean* and the White Mountains tastes simply fabulous. But you should allow yourself to

The island's rich history is incorporated in modern life almost coincidentally

be beamed back 3500 years, if only for a day: when you visit the Iráklio Archaeological Museum and the palace town of *Knossós*, just a few miles from there. Then even an amateur will understand why the Cretans only smile weakly when they hear the Americans speak of their "history": here in Knossós, people in the prehistoric times were already living in five-storey houses, creating art and utility items that still delight us today.

However, it is unlikely to have been for them that any of the 3.5 million-plus visitors flew to the island in 2016. The biggest *attractions are the beaches*. Whether sand or shingle, the island has it all. Often miles long, as at Georgioúpoli and Réthimno, where the sandy beach starts in the middle of the town. Sometimes

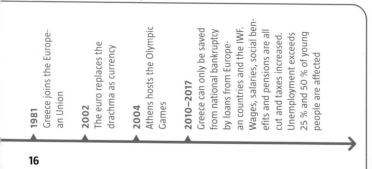

1981
Greece joins the European Union

2002
The euro replaces the drachma as currency

2004
Athens hosts the Olympic Games

2010–2017
Greece can only be saved from national bankruptcy by loans from European countries and the IWF. Wages, salaries, social benefits and pensions are all cut and taxes increased. Unemployment exceeds 25 % and 50 % of young people are affected

with *dunes*, as in Plakiás, or with a *palm grove* such as in Vai. *Party beaches* such as the one at Mália, tiny bays like those at Xerókambos, where no one minds how little you are wearing. Beaches with endless beach furniture and sun shades, bars and *water sports station*. And then more isolated strips of shingle or sand against steep cliffs and sandy slopes. Whatever your dream beach, you're sure to find it on Crete. Some have already been voted the loveliest in Europe by magazines and the social media: the *South Sea-like lagoons* of Elafonísi and Bálos to the far west, *Préveli Beach* against a palm canyon to the south of the island. And then there are the three tiny islands off Crete, which you can *visit for the day by boat*: Gávdos is the *southernmost island of Europe*, Chrisí off Ierápetra and *Koufonísi*, where an ancient theatre is slowly sinking into the fine sand. None of the beaches are off-limits to visitors, because visitor's taxes and private beaches are not an issue for the freedom-loving Cretans.

The palm grove on the beach at Vai, which is rarely this quiet, is lovely but out of bounds

Admittedly, you can find good beaches all over the world. However, there aren't many places where the mountainworld is *as close to the sea* as on Crete. Enticing visitors away from the beach to other activities. There are over 100 unspoilt gorges to explore, some even suitable for school-age children, while others require some climbing experience. Those who are brave enough can leap 100 m/328 ft down into the Arádena Gorge on a *bungee*. *Stalactite caves* are waiting to be explored, 2000-m/660-ft mountains to be climbed. And wherever you go, all the cosy little *mountain villages* have their kafenía, where interested locals

> **There are more than 100 wild gorges to explore**

will be happy to make your acquaintance. And those are the places where you will realise that most Cretans cherish their optimism and their *composure* – even in these times of the crisis in Greece. All things considered, life hasn't been too bad over the past 3500 years. Politicians come and politicians go, but none of them are going to spell the end for Crete …

WHAT'S HOT

1 Ancient craft meets new design

Arts and crafts The designs are extravagant, the techniques are traditional. Cretan artists are rediscovering old techniques. Like Manólis Patramánis of *Virus Ceramicus* (*Odós K. Kipréou 9 | Iráklio | www.virusceramicus.com*), who has devoted himself to modern ceramics. His favourite objects are lips, monks and angels. By contrast, *Níkos Ploumákis* in the large pottery village of *Thrapsanó (www.e-thrapsano.gr)* is dedicated entirely to the ancient Minoan shapes. Works by the progressive glass artists Mario Chalkiadáki and Natássa Papadogamvráki of *Tarrha Glass* (*Anógia | www.tarrhaglass.com*) (photo) have already managed to get as far as museums.

Daily soap in Aegean

TV series The Cretans are no more willing than anybody else to miss their favourite series if they don't have to, and more and more of them are now being filmed in Greek. The good people of Hellas are not interested in Good Times, Bad Times. Clever, sophisticated dialogue is called for, along with real Greek topics, conflicts and dramas. In the comedy series *Eptá thanássimes petherés* (Seven Deadly Mothers-in-Law), for instance, every episode recaps just what a mama will do to keep her mama's boy (or girl) for herself. Certainly unconventional! And the more dramatic *To Nisí* (The Island) even tells the story of the Cretan leprosy island *Spinalónga*. A trans-Aegean relationship is confirmed by the huge success of the Turkish soap opera about Sultan Süleyman the Magnificent, where the Cretans even start to take note of a ruler who seriously suppressed their ancestors.

Outdoor living

Roof terraces Flat roofs are the norm in the towns of Crete, but in the past were rarely used. With their solar systems, water containers and air conditioners, they often looked ugly and unappealing. Howerver, today they are increasingly being used as an additional living area – that is to say, roof terraces. Tables, chairs, swing seats, sun umbrellas and a few plants, and you have a heavenly outdoor spot of your own for very little money. The rooftop bars that are also seen increasingly on roofs offer some lovely insights into theser "home extensions". Two particularly successful such ventures are the *Chez Georges (Odós V. Kornarou 2 | www.chezgeorges.gr)* café bar in Ágios Nikólaos, and *Brascos Bar (Odós Moátsu ke Damianú 1 | www.brascos.com)* on the hotel of the same name in Réthimno.

3

Happy without meat

Veggie cuisine In these times of various crises, many Cretans are also opting for a healthier lifestyle. At home they have always preferred to eat vegetables, legumes and little fishies anyway. But now empty wallets are forcing them to omit the meat when dining in tavernas as well. However, entirely meat-free are only the *Third Eye (thirdeye-paleochora.com)* in Paleochóra and *Kofinas (To Stáchi) (Odos Defkalíonos 5)* in the old town of Chaniá, but more and more establishments are offering meat-free versions of typical Cretan dishes. So, increasingly often, tomatoes and peppers such as they are served at the *Vegera Taverna (www.vegerazaros.gr)* in the mountain village of Záros will conceal an interior of rice and herbs, and meat-free alternatives to the stuffings in vine or cabbage leaves are also frequently available.

4

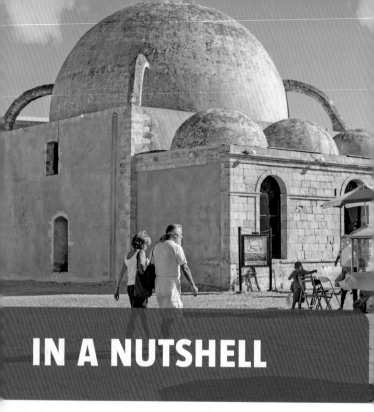

IN A NUTSHELL

BYZANTINE

Do you like to understand what you are reading? On Crete, you'll see thousands of mostly brown signs with the English word "Byzantine" on them. This is a reference to the Byzantine era, from around 500 to 1453 AD, so roughly around the time of our Middle Ages. Crete belonged to the Byzantine Empire until 1204. This empire covered all Asia Minor, the Balkans and Greece. The capital was Constantinople, which the Turks renamed Istanbul after they conquered it in 1453.

Many Greeks would like it to be changed back. Listen closely to airport announcement in Iráklio: Turkish Airlines flies to "Konstantinoupolis". And many Cretan monasteries and churches in particular still fly the yellow-and-black flag of Byzantium. After all, it is where the Orthodox patriarch, the counterpart to the Catholic Pope, still resides.

ANAGRAMS

The Cretans hate rules and regulations. They're not interested in the Greek dictionary. And that can sometimes make foreigners despair. Even in Greek, the names of many towns and villages may be spelt differently on signposts and maps. And even more so when it comes to the Latin alphabet. "Agia", for instance, which means "Saint". Sometimes it's "Agía", as used by Marco Polo, other times it's "Aghia" or "Ayia". All three versions are correct. if you don't have many rules, you won't make many mistakes. All we can do is be resourceful.

Romans and Venetians, Turks, tourists and tomato growers – despite many invaders the island has preserved its own unique character

THE DUTCH – WHO ELSE?

What's that glittering over there? Many of the island's coastal plains sparkle in the sun like vast lakes when you look down on them. This is due primarily to The Netherlands. Of course, it was a Dutchman who, in the early 1960s, showed the Cretans how to grow tomatoes, fruit and vegetables in greenhouses. Thanks to the Cretan sun, there's no need for expensive heating for them. Although the farmers earn good money from the thermokípia, all the environment gets is rubbish. That's because they're covered in plastic film rather than glass, and once that becomes useless, it is shredded by the wind and blows away: waste disposal, Greek-style.

KRÍSIS

The word "krísis" ("crisis" in English) has been on every Creton's lips since 2010. It has become the normal state, indeed normal life. People are dealing with the tax increases and pension reductions, with the lack of work and perspective.

Flower beds are being turned into vegetable plots, and people are heating more with wood than with oil or electricty. In the tavernas, unlike the "olden days", people are only ordering what they can eat. Instead of spending 93 minutes (which has been proven statistically!) over a cup of coffee, people are now spending three hours with it. And they are helping each other with the olive and grape harvests instead of employing Eastern Europeans. They're managing to get by – as long as the tourists keep coming.

STRANGE SOUNDS?

Young Cretans' taste in mustic is just as trendy as that of their contemporaries in the rest of Europe. And still, most of them are just as fascinated by *lýra* and *laoúto* as their grandparents were. The three-stringed pear-shaped lyre and the laoúto, a five-stringed plucked instrument, fills half of all of the music programmes on the radio, and can be heard in numerous tavernas. In fact, they even occasionally make it into the clubs.

Mostly the lyre players celebrate a kind of monotonous speech song called, *mantinádes* and *rizítika*, with their music. Although there are classics, texts are also often improvised for a specific situation and for those present. So if you're in a taverna and everyone suddenly turns around to look at you, it's quite possible that you're currently the subject of some gentle teasing.

MORE THAN A DALLIANCE

Life was pretty exciting in the ancient world of the gods. One drama followed

Trekking through the dry landscape of the Psiloritis mountain range with donkeys and ponies in tow

the next, and not always suitable for young eyes. Zeus, the father of the gods, abducted Europa, the underaged daughter of the Phoenician king to Crete, and produced Mínos, its first king, with her. His wife Pasiphae burned with lust for a white bull. She had an animate wooden cow wrapped in bovine skin made and concealed herself inside it. The bull fell for this trick, and the queen conceived a hybrid child, a monster, the legendary minotaur. Mínos had the beast locked up in a labyrinth, where it was regularly fed young Athenian men and virgins. The Athenian hero Theseus killed the bull and, using Ariadne's thread, even managed to find his way out of the labyrinth. He took Ariadne home with him. But on a stopover on the island of Naxos, Dionysos, the god of wine and theatre, spotted the pretty girl and immediately married her. Theseus continued without her, but set black sails. These were misinterpreted by his father, the Athenian King Aegeus, who then threw himself into the sea in despair. Since then, this sea has been called the Aegean Sea.

Play me! Cretan music would not be the same without the *lýra*

ENTÁXI AND ENTÉCHNO

When a Cretan says *entáxi*, he is saying "ok" rather than asking for a taxi. *Entéchno* is a similar trap – and as a music style, is on everyone's lips. However, it has absolutely nothing to do with techno. Entéchno refers to rocky ballads with Greek texts, usually performed by a soloist accompanied just by a guitar. And you don't have to be a techno freak to enjoy it.

RARELY ALONE

Cretans don't like being alone. And cosy togetherness is only appreciated when whispering sweet nothings, otherwise *paréa* is the order of the day, companionship. That's what they take for coffee or a meal, to a club dancing, on holiday. And the question that is asked later is never about the quality of the hotel or food, but whether the *paréa* was good. And on the rare occasions when people do have to be alone – perhaps in the car, at the cash desk or in the fields – they still have the saints. They are always present everywhere in the form of icons, whether painted or only printed. And of course, they're also in the many churches, chapels and numerous picture sticks on the roadsides. So they can rest assured that they're always well protected and in good company.

SCHNAPPS AS A CULTURAL HERITAGE

Ouzo is elsewhere. People drink rakí on Crete, which is distilled around the clock in October and November in hundreds of tiny distilleries in villages and olive groves. Often made without additives, only from the fermented mash that is left over after the grapes have been pressed for wine. Guest-

WEBSITE WAS YESTERDAY

Cretan websites are often poorly maintained with little information. Well, it's hard work, a website. That's why many

Every town has a church – testimony to the strong Greek Orthodox faith

houses, holiday apartments and hotels frequently leave a small caraffe of rakí in guests' rooms on arrival. Hosts are extremely generous with it, often giving diners a free caraffe of it with dessert, also free – sometimes even doing so at breakfast.

And they can afford to be generous with it, because to date the tax on the Cretan national drink, which is very similar to Italian grappa, is very low. Very much to the annoyance of the politicians in Brussels, who demand it should be taxed the same as ouzo and whisky. The Cretans are vehemently opposed to this: they consider this free use of it as a world heritage.

landlords have moved to Facebook & co. instead, with almost all events now only being posted there. Hoteliers would rather pay commissions of up to 20% to booking.com and airbnb.com than use professional agenies for their URL. More and more private persons have accounts on Facebook, instagram and Linkedin, too. Just type in "crete" or "kriti" and wait for the seemingly endless *loading more results*.

LONG HAIR AND BEARDS

It's the way it is: Orthodox priests always wear their dark robes. Even when they go shopping or for a walk with their wives and children. They are allowed to marry; celibacy is only required for bishops and above. But there are three other things the *pappás* has to have: a stiff hat, long hair and a long beard. Usually the dear Lord protects them agains losing their hair. *Pappádes* are a common sight, even in coffee houses and tavernas. And their jobs are secure; they are paid by the government. There is no church tax in Hellas – so no one ever leaves the church, either. Almost 98% of Cretans are members of the Greek-Orthodox church.

SPARTANS ON THE SKIN

Tattoos are not only popular with the many British visitors to Crete. More and more Cretans are also having images permanently applied to their skin. As they don't weigh anything, they make popular souvenirs. How about a Greek letter on your back, or a caraffe of rakí on your arm? Ghostly pirate ships, Spartan warriors, the philosopher Aristotle in front of the Acropolis in Athens and Greek sayings are currently among the hits at studios like *Black Sheep* in Chaniá or *Dreamcatcher* in Kókkini Cháni.

NO NEED TO RUSH INTO ANYTHING

No one knows what tomorrow will bring. And the Cretans certainly don't. Nor do they make any long-term predictions. Which is why many major events and festivals – which we usuallly start planning at least a year in advance – are only mentioned a few days before they take place. You'll often only find timetables and museum opening times in the internet when they've been valid for a few days. The Cretans even like to be a little vague when making personal arrangements. They'll arrange to meet in the morning or afternoon, evening or next week, and always add a *ta léme*: "We'll talk again".

An hour before you're due to meet is still time enough to agree an exact time. Plus or minus half an hour, of course!

LOOK, THERE THEY ARE!

Vultures are also seen as animals in Europe. They can be recognised by their tremendous wingspan as they circle in the sky. The roughly 300 griffon vultures on Crete have a wingspan of up to 2.60 m/8.5 ft across, while the last ten (give or take) Cretan bearded cultures measure an impressive 3 m/9.8 ft. The best places to watch them gliding in the sky is in the gorges to the west of the island. Crete's three types of eagle are even rarer than vultures: golden eagle, osprey and sea eagle. For excellent information on all these birds of pry go to *www.crete-birding.co.uk*.

BUILDING INSTEAD OF SAVING

Are the Greeks really so badly off? The numerous lovely houses and expensive cars would suggest otherwise. But things aren't as they seem: all the luxury goods were acquired before the crisis – although that doesn't mean they were all paid for. Banks were calling private individuals almost weekly to persuade them to take out loans. People who only wanted 20,000 euros found themselves with 50,000 euros. Spending instead of scrimping was the order of the day on the financial market. Now many Cretans are stuck with their debts. And the supposed securities on which the banks had been counting are no more. They don't even want to seize the goods. Because with such an abundance of high-debt houses, olive groves and fields, the individual ones are really not worth a lot – and only a few ordinary people have enough money to buy them off the banks.

FOOD & DRINK

"If I want to eat alone, I can stay at home," says almost every Cretan. And before you know it, they have drummed up friends and relations and are headed for the taverna together. Which is why you'll usually only find table for two in the places where the tourists go.

This dining community which the Cretans call *paréa* means that no one orders just for themselves. Instead a variety of salads and delicious starters are ordered and everyone then helps themselves. Then large platters of *fish or grilled meat* are ordered which are also put on the table for everyone to share. Most Cretans do without dessert, because the portions are so generous there are usually a lot of leftovers. It is not the done thing to clear the platters and plates completely as this is taken as being miserly.

As a tourist dining out alone or with a partner, you can of course order in the normal fashion – although the Cretan way is much more fun and you get to sample a *variety of dishes*. If the waiter does not clear away your plates as you dine it is because this is a sign to show the other diners that you can afford a lavish meal. By the way: it is the Cretan custom that *one person usually pays for everyone*, if this does not suit you then let the waiter know when you place your order.

In the holiday resort areas Cretans have adapted to the customs of the holiday-makers by decorating the tavernas in

Photo: Mezé – lots of small dishes

Food the Cretan way: good dining in Crete means easy going conviviality around a large table

the traditional way and bringing the food to the table hot. In recent years a number of restaurants have opened that serve haute cuisine. Their main clientele are the Cretans themselves but also Greek holidaymakers who value *good regional cuisine*.

So, everyone finds what they are looking for: from simple, inexpensive little snack bars for *gyros* and *souvláki* to upmarket Italian restaurants with Mediterranean cuisine, from simple family tavernas with *home cooking* to Cretan *gourmet restaurants* with exquisite creations. No matter where you eat, if you order fresh fish, be prepared to pay high prices: you will not find anything under 40 euros per kilo.

When dining out, Cretans drink water and beer or wine. A wide variety of Cretan wines are available and the quality has improved substantially in recent years. Aside from wine by the glass and the affordable *rétsina* – Greek white wine infused with resin from the Aleppo pine – there are also a large

LOCAL SPECIALITIES

apékia – pork casserole dish

briám – oven baked aubergines and olive oil

choriátiki – Greek tomato salad served with goat's cheese and olives

chtapódi – squid, grilled, braised or as a cold salad

dákos – the Cretan variation of bruschetta: finely chopped tomatoes, herbs, onions and oil served on toasted bread (photo right)

dolmádes – vine leaves filled with rice and minced meat, served hot with a béchamel sauce (photo left)

fakí – lentil soup

fasoláda – bean soup

fáva – pureed yellow peas which the guests prepare themselves at the table with onions and olive oil

gópes – grilled sardines

jemistés – tomatoes and peppers filled with rice and minced meat

juvétsi – noodles with beef or lamb baked in an earthenware pot

kakaviá – fish soup – guests choose their own fish

kalitsúnia – pastry filled with spinach or chard and cream cheese

ksifía – grilled swordfish

kúklus – boiled snails accompanied by a glass of rakí

lachanodolmádes – small cabbage rolls filled with rice, minced meat and herbs and served with a béchamel sauce

marídes – crispy fried anchovies

moussaká – baked dish of minced meat, aubergines, potatoes and béchamel sauce

paidákia – grilled lamb chops – best over wood coals

pantsária – red beetroot, either served cold as a salad or hot with its leaves as a vegetable

pastítsjo – baked dish made of macaroni, minced meat and béchamel sauce

patsá – tripe soup

revithókeftédes – potato pancakes or croquettes made from chickpea flour

Sfakiániés píttes – a type of crêpe, filled with honey and cream cheese

sínglino – lightly smoked pork

stifádo – mostly beef (sometimes rabbit) stew in a tomato and cinnamon sauce with vegetables

supjés – a type of squid

number of quality wines from larger or smaller cellars. Wines from the *co-operative wine cellars* of Sitía and Péza near Iráklio are recommended. There are also some more exclusive wines in limited quantities available from independent cellars like *Lýrarákis*, *Económou*, *Manoussákis*, *Michalákis* and *Crétas Olympías*. *Boutáris* is a quality wine produced throughout Greece.

Most tavernas and restaurants are open from 9am until *well after midnight*. Cretans seldom eat lunch before 1pm and at night you will find them with their *paréa* dining at 10pm or even later.

Lovers of sweet delicacies can visit a *zacharoplastío,* the Greek version of a confectionery. Here you will find a wide variety of tarts, pastries, pralines and oriental pastries like *baklavá* and *kataifi*, which look sweeter than they actually are, and the favourite *milópita* (apple pie) which is often served with vanilla ice cream.

Cretan coffee houses are where the men meet. Every village has at least one *kafenío*, most have more *kafenía*. This is necessary because each *kafenío* is associated with one of the three main Greek political parties: the Conservatives, the Socialists or the Communists. Although operated by a private owner, the *kafenío* is something of a public institution. There is usually no obligation to order anything. The men sit down together to talk about God and the world and above all about Greek politics or to play *távli*, draughts or cards.

When you order a coffee for yourself, remember to say exactly how you prefer it. The Cretans drink *Greek coffee* which is coffee brewed together with water and sugar. *Kafé ellinikó* is served in many variations: *skétto*, without sugar; *métrio*, with some sugar; *glikó*, with

Typically Cretan: mocha with a glass of water

lots of sugar; *dipló*, a double portion. Instant coffee is also always available. Basically you order it as *neskafé* and specify the amount of sugar you prefer. There is also the option of *neskafé sestó*, hot or *frappé*, cold Nescafé beaten to foam.

Young Cretans love cold variants of coffee like *freddo espresso* and *freddo cappuccino*, and just like the Greek espresso, they are served with a glass of cold water.

SHOPPING

In the souvenir shops in the cities and resorts you will find lots of mass-produced goods that are seldom made in Crete. It is better to shop in the alleyways of Chaniá and Réthimno, the shops in Ágios Nikólaos, the crafters' workshops on roadsides and in the villages.

Shop hours: in resort areas and during the peak season usually daily 10am–midnight, in the cities Mon–Sat 10am–1.30pm, Tue, Thu and Fri also 5.30pm–8pm.

ARTS & CRAFTS

Coloured glass is a craft on the rise and there are glass artists everywhere in Greece. The large glassworks in Kókkino Chorió, 26 km/15.2 mi east of Chaniá, is famous for its articles made from recycled glass. You will also find modern and traditional ceramics all over Crete. Margarítes, 27 km/16.8 mi south-east of Réthimno, is a potters' village well worth visiting. Carvings from olive wood are particularly valuable because the wood has to be cured for a long time and is very difficult to work with. The largest selection can be found in Mátala on the southern coast.

Not made of olive wood but great fun: the wooden, hand-painted men's bow-ties and sunglasses frames that you can buy in Iráklio.

CULINARY DELIGHTS

Olives, olive oil and honey are healthy souvenirs which can also be bought in the many trendy health food shops. Fruit preserves, dried fruit and the many types of cheese are also typical of the island.

FASHION

Cretan fashionistas fly to Athens for their shopping; only Iráklio offers a few international labels in the town centre. High-quality T-shirts and children's clothing from their own Cretan production are available from Ágios Nikólaos.

JEWELLERY

In Crete you will still find some small gold and silversmiths – who still produce some of their wares themselves – e.g. in Chaniá's old town and the harbour at Ágios Nikólaos. Before you buy, always check the quality. It is best to de-

Mainstream is all over the island. But when you know where to look, you'll also find the original in Crete's towns

cline the glass of *oúzo* offered by the salespersons.

LEATHER

Chaniá is the island's leather centre. Skrídloff is a long street that sells masses of bags and accessories "Made in Greece" (or Italy). Not necessarily the place for *Georgína Skalídi*. Her luxurious bags are artistic one-offs, and available exclusively from her boutique in Chaniá.

MUSEUM REPLICAS

Seldom do you find as many museum objects as in Crete but only a few will be authorised copies. The museum shop in the Venetian loggia in Réthimno offers the widest variety and they also ship larger objects anywhere in the world. A few jewellers opposite the Archaeological Museum in Iráklio also sell good (but unauthorised) copies of Minoan jewellery.

MUSIC

Whether it is traditional Cretan *lýra* sounds or the rock music of the Greek charts – you will find them in any music shop in Crete.

SHOES

When it comes to their footwear, the ladies of Crete really like to go mad. A shoemaker in Iráklio takes the (shoe) biscuit: he customises shoes to his clients' wishes– within 48 hours if required.

SPIRITS & WINE

A good selection of Cretan wines are available in the cities from the speciality shops called *cáva*. Especially the wine cellars Péza and Boutáris close to Iráklio offer wine tastings and direct purchases. *Rakí* can be bought everywhere but because the quality differs it is better to sample it before you buy.

CHANIÁ

Born to be wild? Then West Crete is the perfect holiday region for you. The White Mountains contain almost more gorges than villages, while between the rough cliff faces of the Libyan Sea are isolated beaches and only a very few tiny villages.

Some of them you can only get to by boat. In the South Sea-like lagoons on the extreme west you'll swim in turquoise waters, while in the protected valleys you can literally pick oranges straight from the trees. Sheep graze between ancient ruins, while the Middles Ages surround you in the old town of Chaniá. You won't find most of the bathing resorts in this part of the island in any of the package holidays brochures – they're mostly for individualists.

CHANIÁ

MAP INSIDE BACK COVER
(143 E3) (_M D2_) Chaniá itself is worth a few days of your holiday; of all the Cretan towns, it is the Beauty Queen. Boredom is unheard of in the island's second-largest town (pop. 108,000).

In the mornings, museums with plenty of maritime touches; lunch in the *harbour*, wellness in the oriental hammam. Then some relaxed, exclusive shopping. Followed by dinner in the old Turkish baths. Then a carriage ride, first some traditional lyre music, and later on jazz until sunrise – that would be a good programme. Wouldn't it? You

White Mountains, steep coasts: hike through the Iríni Gorge or take a boat out to the islands and coves in the diverse west

CITY **WHERE TO START?**
Old town: Parking close to the old town is scarce. The best option is at the north-western harbour exit at the platía Taló. Municipal buses stop at the market hall. The terminal for long distance buses is close to Platía 1866, from where the old town and harbour is just a five minute walk away.

won't have to leave the ⭐ *old town*, which is much shaped by the Venetians, for it, either, as the new town has nothing to offer apart from the entertaining park. Nor does history abandon you when you sleep, because many of the houses in the old town are now tiny boutique hotels and guesthouses with style. They often have a roof garden, from where you can see the vast Aegean and the almost 2500 m/8200 ft high peaks. Their tips are snow-covered from the end of October until May!

SIGHTSEEING

ÁGIOS NIKÓLAOS CHURCH

You won't see this anywhere else: a church with a minaret! When the Turks conquered Crete in 1669, they converted many of the Christian churches into Islamic places of prayer. All they had to do was remove the icons, paint over or scrape off the murals, install a prayer recess facing Mecca, and place a minaret on top. After 1913, these mosques were

the museum's (free) brochure. It is of a monumental lance bearer on the rooftops of Minoan Chaniá. *April–Oct daily from 8am–8pm, Nov–Mar Tue–Sun 8am–3pm | admission 4 euros | Odós Chalidón 25*

HARBOUR ⭐

A blessing in disguise: because the harbour in Chaniá is so silted up, the only boats that can enter are fishing boats and yachts. This means that the long harbour quay is almost traffic-free, which

Minoan artistry: painted sarcophagi in the Archaeological Museum

then turned back into churches. All the other minarets were removed, but this one was eventually restored. That's tolerance for you. *Platía 1821*

ARCHAEOLOGICAL MUSEUM

Crete's loveliest museum is a Gothic church from Venetian times. The most interesting things about it are the primitive hunting scenes on sarcophagi that are over 3300 years old. A tiny seal from the 15th century BC is unique, and can also be seen on

makes it perfect for strolling down. The only vehicles on the tarmac are horse-drawn carriages. Cafés and tavernas nestle cheek by jowl between the *Nautical Museum* and the eye-catching but ugly *Janissary Mosque*. Then it gets quieter: past more or less well-preserved Venetian shipyards and a few basic fish restaurants to the *Minoan ship* and the nighttime party quarter on the east side of the harbour. Then follows a long jetty on which you can walk or jog.

JEWISH QUARTER

Narrow streets, tiny shops, cosy tavernas: the Odós Kondiláki is worth a visit. The town's Jewish community lived here until the Holocaust. All that remains of it is the tiny *synagogue Etz Hayyim (May–Oct Mon–Thu 10am–6pm, Fri 10am–3pm, Nov–Apr Mon–Thu 10am–5pm, Fri 10am–3pm)*, which was a Christian church until 1669. International voluntary guides are available to take you around (for a donation of 2 euros) and will tell you about what happens in a synagogue.

MINOAN SHIP

Would you row from Crete to Piraeus? A Cretan team attempted it in 2004 – and despite the auxiliary sails, it took them 27 days to sail the 390 km/240 mi. What made it even more amazing: the bold men and women were travelling in the same kind of boat as the Minoans would have used for their long-distance sailing expeditions over 3300 years before. Today, this scientifically based reproduction is housed in an old Venetian shipyard, where video films tell you more about the construction and trip of the "Minoa". *May–Oct Mon–Sat 9am–5pm, Sun 10am–6pm | admission 2 euros | Odós Defkalónia*

NAUTICAL MUSEUM

How lovely that models exist. This shipping museum shows us what the town looked like in the year 1600. History lovers in particular will appreciate the re-telling of the historic sea battles with miniature ships; you can even have a close look at a Venetian galley ship. On the top floor, Germans and Austrians are confronted by a dark chapter in their history: the attack on Crete in 1941. *Mon–Sat 9am–3.30pm, Sun 10am–6pm, in winter daily 9am–5pm | ad-mission 3 euros | Aktí Kundurióti | www.mar-mus-crete.gr*

CITY PARK

The Chanioti are almost by themselves in the town's "green lung". Sitting in the chicest, most traditional coffee house on the island, ● *O Kípos (daily from 8am | Moderate)*, playing cards, Távli, Scrabble and Monopoly as they drink their *Kafés ellinikós* or a glass of Champagne. A few steps on, Cretan wild goats with their mighty horns graze quietly – while in the evenings, Hollywood & co. are shown in the summer cinena under the starry sky. *Odós Dimokratías/Odós Tzanakáki*

TOPANÁS

Oh, sweet seduction! Lots of tiny shops and artists' studios have opened up in the old town of Topaná that you'll struggle to resist. Quality and originality about on straight-as-a-die Odós Theotokópoulou and its side streets, and if you climb up the *Schiávo bastion* at the end you'll be able to see over the old town to the sea.

HISTORICAL & FOLK MUSEUM

Do you think museums are dead? Then try this one. You'll see craftsmen sitting in their historic workshops, while a vintner distills *rakí* all year round, and a grandmother shivers by the fire even in summer. The fact that they are all made of wax has the advantage that your photos will be nice and clear. *Mon, Tue, Thu, Fri 9am–6pm, Wed, Sat 9am–5pm, Sun 11am–4pm | admission 3 euros | Odós Chalidón 46b*

FOOD & DRINK

MESOGIAKÓ

In his small, modernly furnished tavern in the old part of the city, restaurateur Michális Pedinákis offers Mediterranean dishes including lamb served without the usual bones. The wide choice of salads is particularly tasty. Homemade pannacotta is the perfect dessert. *Daily from noon | Odós Chatzimicháli Daligiánni 36 | www.mesogiako. com | Moderate*

MONASTIRI

Taverna right on the harbour, serving seasonal and special Cretan dishes like cured pork *sínglino* and onion dishes like *volvoús*, the bulbs of the grape hyacinth, *Daily from 11am | Aktí Tombázi 12 | www.monastiri-taverna.gr | Moderate*

TAMAM

Taverna in what was once a Turkish bath, meeting place of the local intellectuals and artists. The food is a combination of recipes from the two important Greek cities that are now in Turkey, Smýrna (now Izmir) and Constantinople (now Istanbul). *Daily from noon | Odós Zambéliu 49 | www.tamamrestaurant.com | Moderate*

SHOPPING

INSIDER TIP CARMELA

In Carmela Iatrópoulou's tiny shop, you'll have all the time in the world to look around in peace. No single item is in there twice, and everything was made either by the Greek owner herself or by her Greek friends. Whether ceramics, jewellery, mosaic or painting – you won't find anything you see here anywhere else. *Odós Angélu 7*

INSIDER TIP GEORGÍNA SKALÍDI

Post-modern clutches are this designer's passion, and she designs all her exemplary bags herself in coloured leather. Even her website is enough to kindle your appetite for them, and you can still that appetete at surprisingly affordable prices. *Mon–Sat 11am–2pm, Tue, Thu, Fri also 6-9pm | Odós Chatzimicháli Dalagiánni 58 | www.georginaskalidi.com*

MUNICIPAL MARKET

This century old building now also has souvenir sellers mixed in with the greengrocers and fishmongers. The most traditional and original aspect of the market are its quaint tavernas. *Mon, Wed, Sat 8.30am–5pm, Tue, Thu, Fri 8.30am–9.30pm | Platía Venizélos*

SPORTS & BEACHES

The beach to the west of the old town may well suffice for a quick dip in

Dine at sunset on Chaniá's old streets – that's the Mediterranean way

between, but for a long day's swimming you'd do better to take the public bus to *Stavrós* on the Akrotíri peninsula. You can actively experience Chaniá by day and night on a *Segway (39–60 euros / 75–120 min | Odós Ep. Chrisánthou 25 | tel. 69 44 59 7159 | www.chaniasegway tours.com)*. Oriental wellness welcomes you at the *Al Hammam* (see p. 121).

ENTERTAINMENT

There's plenty going on in the old town all year round. The standard discos beloved by the happy-drinker tourists are just behind the Janissary Mosque in the harbour on the short Odós Sourméli. The *Klik Bar* is always popular. The local in crowd prefers to meet in the music clubs on the eastern side of the harbour behind the striking Hotel Porto Vene-

ziano. For those with slightly different tastes in music, a jazz club and numerous tavernas with Cretan lyre music open their doors.

CHALKÍNA ●

Sorbás in your blood? Greek and Cretan live music is played daily at this modern Ouzerí in the harbour, at weekends in winter from 10pm. Mainly locals gather here. *Aktí Tombázi 29–30 | www.chal kina.com*

FAGOTTO ●

If you'd rather leave the rocking to others and prefer instead to enjoy good, solid jazz and rock in a cosy bar or down a narrow street in the old town, then the relaxed, well-established Fagotto is your musical home from home. *Daily 9pm–5am | Odós Ángelou 16*

Appealing ruins: in Áptera you'll find antique things and the ruins of an ancient monastery in your picnic area

WHERE TO STAY

DOMUS RENIER

In 2016, two award-winning Cretan architects transformed this tiny aristocratic residence from the 15th century into a boutique hotel with nine rooms and suites for 2–6 people. Renaissance and modernity coexist happily here in the old harbour. The Master Apartment at the top measures an impressive 970 ft². *9 rooms and suites | Aktí Koundourióti 41 | tel. 28 21 08 88 01 | www.domusrenier.gr | Moderate–Expensive*

KASTELI

These six studios and apartments (accommodating up to six people each) are situated in the old town. Decorated with light wood and Cretan tapestry some of them are in a lovely courtyard and they all have an authentic Chaniá atmosphere. *Odós Kanaváro 39 | tel. 28 21 05 70 57 | www.kastelistudios-crete. com | Moderate*

INSIDER TIP KIARA

The four roomy studios that brought a fresh breeze into an old town house were completed in 2016. A kitchenette with an espresso machine and small balcony are standard features, while the studio on the top of the three floors even has its own roomy terrace. *4 apts. | Odós Theotokópoulou 50 | tel. 69 73 24 49 45 | www. studioskiara.com | Moderate–Expensive*

INFORMATION

MUNICIPAL TOURIST INFORMATION
Odós Milonogiánni 53 | town hall | tel. 28 21 34 16 65 | www.chania.gr
Mid June–Sep also information kiosks to the south of the market hall and north of the Janissary Mosque

WHERE TO GO

AKROTÍRI PENINSULA ★
(144 A–B 1–2) (*∅ D–E 1–2*)
Move among monasteries and military cannons here: NATO uses its rocket-

INSIDER TIP ÁPTERA
(144 B2) *(₥ D2)*

Romantic ruins will draw you to the rocky plateau near the coast. In spring, you'll share the tiers of the ancient theatre with scarlet poppies. A round of applause is also due to the backdrop of the White Mountains against green valleys. Check out your echo in one of the two vast Roman cisterns, then unpack your picnic in the courtyard of a Medieval abbey. The attendant limits his activities to his job at the ticket desk; no one will stifle your thirst for research *(Tue–Sun 8am–3pm | admission 3 euros)*. As you continue on the short drive to the Ottoman fort on the steep slope of the plateau, you'll come across the remains of the once miles-long town wall and pass fields full of giant fennel, which the earlier fishermen and sailors used as fire lighters: Break open one of the dried stalks (which grow to lengths of up to 2 m/6.6 ft) in late summer or autumn, and you can make the pulp in them glow. Just hold a cigarette lighter or match to it, blow for a few seconds, and you'll have a glimmer. Which is exactly how Prometheus first brought fire to mankind on earth. *16 km/9.9 mi*

firing base on the peninsula for firing away taxes, while the monks in two monasteries pray for peace. And although you can only see the military barracks from a distance, you are welcome to visit the monasteries. The monks at *Agía Triáda (daily from 9am–6pm | admission 2 euros)* work busily producing olive oil, wine and schnapps. You can also visit the wine cellar with the adjoining tasting room and the 17th century church with its traditional murals. Prayer and their lovely garden are the main interests of the extremely devout monks at the *Gouvernéto Monastery (Sun 5am–11am and 5pm–8pm, Oct–Easter 4pm–7pm; Mon, Tue, Thu, Sat 10am–1pm and 5pm–6pm | admission free)* of the 16th century, which strongly resembles a desert fort. Modest clothing is essential here. Fancy a little walk? There is a proper path from the Gouvernéto Abbey through the quiet landscape past a chapel in a stalactite cave to the now abandoned *Kathólikó Monastery* beside a gorge. *Round trip approx. 50–60 km/30–37 mi*

BÁLOS BEACH ★ (142 A2) (*ω A1–2*)

Wow! Whether you come on the excursion boat from Kissámos or on foot from the car park at the end of a rough slope, the ☼ views of the lagoon of *Bálos* with its white beaches against the bare cliffs will blow you over. And apart from a single taverna, there are no buildings in sight; not even campers are allowed to stay overnight here. Sailors can also explore the Venetian fortified island of *Gramvoúsa* on the way over. Car drivers and hikers can ride a donkey down from the car park to the beach. Travel here along a 7 km/4.4 mi track that is suitable (with care!) for cars *(toll 2 euros)* from the village of Kaliviani. Boat trips from Kissámos are offered by *Cretan Daily Cruises (daily approx. 9.30am | 2 euros | tel. 28 22 02 43 44 | www.cretan daily cruises.com).*

CHÓRA SFAKÍON (144 B5) (*ω D4*)

Do you love bends? Then you'll travel through paradise when you come here from the northern coast: 20 ● tight hairpin bends take you from the Askífou high plane down to the Libyan Sea and tiny Chóra Sfakíon, which despite having a population of only 265 is nonetheless able to proudly call itself the capital of the Sfakiá. From here there are ferries along the southern coast to *Paleochóra* (see p. 43) that also stop in *Agía Rouméli*, the destination of any hike through the *Samariá Gorge* (see p. 116). Car ferries chug across to ● *Gávdos*, Europe's southernmost island, where you can spend a night under the starry skies. Or a sea taxi will take you to the completely traffic-free bathing resort of *Loutró* (see p. 43), which also has a tiny beach right on the outskirts. So if you'd like to do a lot of hiking and spend a lot of time on the water, this is the perfect place for you to spend a few days – perhaps at the guesthouse *Stavris (34 rooms | tel. 28 25 09 12 20 | www.stavris.com | Budget)* above the harbour. *73 km/45.4 mi*

ELAFONÍSI BEACH ★ (142 A5) (*ω A4*)

Blue, turquoise or green? The still waters on the finest sand shimmer on this beach in every imaginable hue. This has made the beach extremely popular with visitors, especially in high summer. Tavernas and guesthouses have been banished to the hinterland, and watersports are banned. So nature is able to come into its own. Those who would like to have Elafonísi mostly to themselves should stay at the *Panórama (7 rooms | tel. 69 37 29 53 65 | Budget)* or in the neighbouring village of Chrissoskalítissa at the *Glykería (9 rooms | tel. 28 22 06 12 92 | www.glykeria.com | Moderate)*, where the eponymous, blindingly white monastery can also be seen in a highly photogenic position on a rock. *78 km/48.5 mi*

FOURNÉS (143 E4) (*ω C3*)

Could it be any healthier! The ☻ *Taverne* of the 50-acre *Botanical Park of Crete (March–mid-Nov daily from 9am until 75 min before sunset | admission 6 euros | on the road to Ómalos | www.botanical-park.com | Moderate)* serves only freshly-squeezed juices from fruit they harvested themselves. And you can rest assured we're not just talking about the oranges that grow on tens of thousands of trees here in Fournés and the surrounding villages, but also about exotic varieties such as papaya, guavas, passionfruit and kiwis. The kitchen prepares typical Cretan dishes flavoured with local herbs, limes and lemongrass, and bakes its own bread in the wood-fired oven. Not hungry? Then go for a walk along the 3 km/1.9 mi of trails through the Mediterranean and tropical gardens, and we'll talk again. *15 km/9.3 mi*

FRANGOKASTÉLLO ☆
(144 B–C5) (⊞ E4–5)

If you're scared of ghosts, then stay away from this Venetian *castle (daily from 9am–5pm | admission 2 euros)* on 17 May, as that is when it is visited by the spirits of the Cretan freedom fights who in 1828 tried unsuccessfully to en-

studios.net | Budget) right on the beach by the fort. *80 km/49.7 mi*

GEORGIOÚPOLI (144 C3) (⊞ E3)

The mix is right: Georgioúpoli is a typical Cretan village with a perfectly good life of its own, and yet perfectly prepared for holiday-makers. Fishermen still bring

The beach at Elafonisi has the appearance of a South Pacific lagoon and is also perfect for children.

trench themselves here from the Turkish troops. You can safely enter on any other day of the year. Right outside is a wide, extremely flat sandy beach. Around 400 m/1300 ft further east you can tumble down the sandy slope of the Órthi Ámmos beach straight into the deep waters. There are only few buildings along the entire coastal plain, and there is no centre as such – ideal for a relaxed, very quiet holiday. A good place to stay is the *Marias Studios (17 rooms | tel. 28 25 09 21 59 | marias-*

their catches to the river harbour in the mornings, and then head over to the kafenió. Pedalos and kayaks are for hire right under the bridge, which you can take up the river and watch the turtles from. Grannies, grandpas and nursing mums settle down on the modern Platía to watch the tourists.

MTV and Champions League are both shown on the widescreen TVs at the same time. A 14 km/8.7 mi sandy beach starts just to the east of the harbour, and there's still plenty of space between the

Lots of sea and no noise as you dine at quiet, traffic-free Loutró

hotels there. Public buses go to nearby Réthimno and to Chaniá at least every hour, while there are lots of quiet villages in the surrounding area that offer pure rusticity. Mountain bikes are available to hire from *Adventurebikes* (see p. 120) on the street from the Platía to the beach. The three hotels of the *Corissia Group* (265 rooms | tel. 28 25 08 30 10 | www. corissia.com | Budget–Expensive) have integrated perfectly into village life. At night, *Café Titos* on the Platía and the *Beach Bar Tropicana* become clubs, while by day it is easy to get to Lake *Kournás*, which is just 3 km/1.9 mi away. It is the largest mountain lake on the island, and offers a beach, tavernas and pedal boat hire. 40 km/24.9 mi

ÍMBROS GORGE (144 B5) (*Ⓜ E4*)

Glutton or slacker? If you think hiking through the world-famous Samariá Gorge is a little too strenuous, or you have become addicted to gorges, or if you're simply visiting Crete too early or too late in the year, then this easy-to-hike alternative is the solution for you. The Ímbros Gorge is almost as beautiful as its famous sister, but shorter, shallower and not so full. It starts in the village of *Ímbros* on the southern edge of the Askífou high plain, and ends about three hours later in Komitádes. The hosts of the tavernas will organise the transfer to the bus stop in *Chóra Sfakíon* (see p. 40) or back to your car in Ímbros for you. *Open during daytime | admission 2 euros. 57 km/35.4 mi*

INSIDER TIP ▶ IRÍNI GORGE (143 D5) (*Ⓜ B4*)

The Iríni Gorge is just as impressive as the Samariá Gorge but not as well known. The rock faces soar hundreds of metres high and many parts of the gorge are covered in forest and huge boulders lie in the summer dry river bed. The hike starts at the southern edge of the village of *Agía Iríni* on the road from Chaniá to Soúgia. A small forest restaurant is at the entrance. The gorge ends after 7 km/4.4 mi at the simple little INSIDER TIP *Taverna Oásis* (Budget), which fits in perfectly with the landscape. The selection is limited but the food authentic. From here a road continues for 5 km/3.1 mi to Soúgia *(taxi booking tel. 28 23 05 14 84 or tel. 28 23 05 14 85). 56 km/34.8 mi*

KISSÁMOS (142 B3) (*Ø A2*)

Far from the mainstream, you're now in Crete's westernmost little town in the sun. For most visitors to Crete, Kíssamos (pop. 3000) is only the starting point for the boat trip to *Bálos Beach* (see p. 40). The only tourist attraction as such here is the approximately 150-m/500-ft long beach promenade with cafés and tavernas including the *Kelári (Moderate)*. West of that is a good sandy beach, while to the east is a kilometre-long shingle beach. Opposite the *Archaeological Museum (Tue–Sun 8am–3pm | admission 2 euros | Platía Tzanakáki)* with its lovely mosaic floors is the *Strata Tours (Platia Tzanakáki | tel. 28 22 02 42 49 | www. stratatours.com)* travel agency, which hires out bicycles. Owner Stélios goes hiking with visitors, and will even take them into some of the houses in the villages. Stay right on the beach in one of the 32 roomy studios of the *Aphrodite Beach (32 apts. | Odós Agamémnos 49 | tel. 28 22 08 30 99 | aphroditebeach.gr | Budget–Moderate). 42 km/26.1 mi*

LOUTRÓ ★ (144 A5) (*Ø D4*)

Do you yearn for a traffic-free world? Well, your dream can come true in Loutró. The only way to get to this blue-and-white town on the south coast is by boat or on foot; there are no cars. But it does have the INSIDER TIP *Hotel Pórto Loutró (42 rooms/studios | tel. 28 25 09 14 33 | www.hotelportoloutro. com | Moderate)* with basic but extremely pleasant accommodation, several tavernas right on the water's edge and no noise at all. You swim from the rocks and in tiny bays. A 30-minute walk to the completely undeveloped shingle beach of Glikánera, where fresh and salt water mix. *73 km/ 45.4 mi*

MILIÁ ● ◎ (142 B4) (*Ø A3*)

Already in 1982, a few former citizens of the dilapidated mountain village of Miliá decided to renovate the houses as holiday homes and to make them the core of an eco-project that also included agriculture and forestry. This completely car-free village has 13 natural stone houses with Cretan interiors, which are now available as rentals. Water is heated by the sun and comes from a nearby spring, candles and oil lamps are used for light, and the village taverna uses only locally produced organic products *(daily from 8am | tel. 28 21 04 67 74 | www.milia.gr | Moderate). 60 km/37.3 mi*

PALEOCHÓRA (142 B6) (*Ø B4*)

It doesn't get any warmer than this! The large village on the south coast is the warmest place in the whole of Greece. Farmers take advantage of this for the countless solar-heated greenhouses all over the coastal plain. And tourists like it because they can sit outside all night even in spring and autumn. The community and hosts are happy to play along. Every evening at 7, the main street turns into a long *Food Court*, with tavernas, cafés and bars. Just a few steps, and you'll be in the garden of the island's first wine bar, *Monika's Garden (daily from 6pm | on the road from the main junction to the sandy beach | Moderate)*, or you can watch classic films and the latest blockbusters at the *Summer cinema*. There is a long, extra wide sandy beach on one side of the peninsula with the village. The other side will be the choice of people who prefer to lie on shingle. All sorts of boat trips start in the tiny harbour, while quiet mountain villages in the region are good destinations for hikers. The only historical sight in the village is the freely accessible Venetian castle complex ☀ *Kástro Sélino*, which has one main purpose: people meet here at sunset. Night owls usually experience the sunrise at *Ágios Bar* on the main junction in the village. There's plenty of time to go to bed after that: close to the beach is one option, for instance at the hotel *Villa Marise (16 rooms | tel. 28 23 04 11 62 | www.villamarise.com | Budget–Moderate)*. *77 km/47.9 mi*

INSIDER TIP **POLIRRINÍA**
(142 B3) (*Ø A2–3*)
Alone at last! It's unusual to see strangers in this tiny mountain village, which 2500 years ago was an important town. Your best choice is to follow the small signpost to the Acropolis. At the point where the road ends between the walls of the old houses is the medieval church *Ágii Patéres*, with lots of old inscriptions in its exterior walls. They were originally part of a temple, and you can still see the stone blocks used for its supporting walls on the edge of the churchyard, as well as an old circular threshing floor. A 15-minute walk along the narrow footpath will take you through the Macchia and up a rocky hill with all sorts of antique walls along the slopes. The tiny chapel is the perfect place for a picnic in complete isolation. To get back to the village, follow the sign with "O Vráchos" on it, and *Giórgos Tsichlákis* will be waiting for you. The former carpenter sells lovely items made of wood in his studio, including highly imaginative wind chimes, and every October distils his own rakí, which he flavours with his own selections of herbs. You are welcome to sit on his welcoming terrace and sample it, if you like. When you then stroll through the village, you will see other ancient and medieval walls, including the remains of a water system and a

TO EVERY MAN HIS WEAPON

Traffic signs are the favourite targets of some Cretans, which is why at least half of them on the island have holes in them. Stop or no-parking signs with holes in them are evidence of the Cretans' love of liberty. After all, traffic signs are a symbol of authority. According to statistics, every male on the island possesses at least one weapon, and yet violent crime is a rarity. They are fired for joy at weddings and baptisms, or kept in case the Turks come back. The only thing they don't like is seeing policemen with weapons. When in 2011, hundreds of rapid response troops occupied the village of Zonianá in a raid on drug farmers and dealers, the people hit the streets: supposedly the presence of so many armed representatives of authority could endanger children's morality!

Cooking together in the old houses of Vámos makes you feel like a Cretan

cistern from the time of the Roman Emperor Hadrian. *53 km/32.9 mi*

SOÚGIA (142 C6) *(ᗐ B4)*

There isn't much to say about Soúgia, which is precisely why regulars keep returning there every year. No other towns or villages as far as the eye can see; nothing worth visiting, no "you've-simply-got-to-see-this" pressures. With a crystal-clear conscience, you can focus entirely on enjoy the long shingle beach, the mix of Cretan and Alsatian cuisine served at the Ómikron *(Moderate)*, meet other Soúgia fans at the Lotos Music Café next door, and perhaps agree to share a sea taxi with them to a nearby beach. You can even stay with one of the maritime taxi drivers: Captain George *(12 rooms | Tel. 28 23 05 11 33 | www.sougia.info | Budget)*. *70 km/43.5 mi*

VÁMOS ★ ● (144 B3) *(ᗐ E3)*

If gentle tourism is just your thing, you should rent a village house through *Vamos Traditional Village (tel. 28 25 02 21 90 |* *www.vamosvillage.gr | Moderate–Expensive)* in Vámos (pop. 700). You'll quickly become part of the lively village, find yourself sitting amongst the locals on the (not yet traffic-free) Platía, and on your second visit will already be greeted like close friends. In 1995, a group of young people in the large main town on the Apokóronas peninsula had the idea of restoring empty old houses and renting them out. Above an old cistern on the main street is the taverna *Stérna tou Bloumósifis (daily from 11am | Moderate)*, which serves creative Cretan cuisine. The group also owns the travel agency on Vámos' old main street, which as well as providing accommodation also arranges guided hikes, cooking courses and agricultural activities, visits to wineries and cheese dairies. However, you'll need a car, because it's 7 km/4.4 km to the next beach, the *Almirída Beach*. The only buses to the beach and Chaniá go early in the morning and at lunchtime. *22 km/13.7 mi*

RÉTHIMNO

Double the fun. In Réthimno and the surrounding area, you will almost always
have not one, but two high mountain
ranges in your sight: the White Mountains and the Ída Mountains. The two
biggest island towns, Iráklio and Chaniá,
are both only about an hour from Réthimno. And the road between the north and
south coasts is extremely well developed
Which means you can swim both in the
Aegean and in the Libyan Sea. There are
pretty villages in the mountainous hinterland of the town where you can easily spend half or even a whole day. The
large hotel complexes are mainly along
the 16-km/9.9-mi sandy beach of Réthimno, whereas if you stay on the south
coast you are more likely to be in a small
hotel or guesthouse.

RÉTHIMNO

MAP INSIDE BACK COVER
(145 D–E3) (*M F3*) Réthimno (pop.
55,500) is just good fun! A 16-km/
9.9-mi sandy beach with lots of water
sports options starts right on the edge of
the old town – which, with its numerous
minarets and mosques, narrow streets
and tiny squares, Venetian harbour and
castle, is not just a lovely option if you're
dealing with a case of sunburn.

There are endless shops and tavernas,
and lots of pretty little streets take you
through residential areas with little houses and the typical Turkish timber gaze-
bos. And you won't have to spend long
looking for good cocktail bars and clubs

Historical flair: here you can combine sunbathing with journeys of discovery along the enchanted paths of the past

in the evenings; that's taken care of by the town's student scene. Public buses travel to many other towns and beaches in the environment, while cruises along the coast start from the romantic harbour. So boredom is something you will definitely not have to contend with in Réthimno.

Réthimno is dominated by holidaymakers keen to spend time in the (often excellent) hotels close to the beach and only come to town to eat or shop, as well as those who prefer to stay in the histor-

ic old town in cosy guest houses or the modern urban hotels (which are nonetheless well adapted for their surroundings). For both types, the city has its attraction.

Réthimno has a number of cultural activities. The University of Crete has a campus here (as well as in Iráklio and Chaniá) and it is also home to the Philosophy Faculty – the city has seen itself as the intellectual centre of the island for a long time. Réthimno also has a theatre, a philharmonic society and an adult education

Guarded by three lions: It is clear who held power at the time when the Rimóndi fountain was built

college exclusively for women. During the summer months there are guest performances by local and foreign music and theatre groups.

SIGHTSEEING

ARCHAEOLOGICAL MUSEUM

So just what is a loo seat doing in this museum? You'll find out in this little archaeological exhibition in an old Venetian church: this particular one is over 1400 years old, made of stone, and was used for raising boat anchors that had stuck fast. Far more aesthetic are the painted sarcophagi that date back to Minoan times. Try to find the naked youth attempting to slay a boar with his sword. *Tue–Sun 10am–6pm | admission 2 euros | Odós Ethn. Antistáseos*

FORTÉZZA ☆

Time to catch your breath! Only the outer walls are left of the 16th century Venetian castle. Inside, nature has reclaimed the vast plateau at the tip of the town peninsula. A chapel, a mosque and a few cisterns are the only historic traces that remain. The open-air stage is used for concerts and plays in summer – if there's enough money left in the town's coffers, that is. *May–Oct daily from 8.30am–8pm | admission free*

MUSEUM OF CONTEMPORARY ART OF CRETE

The island's best art museum not only has works by Cretan artists of the past 50 years, but also provides plenty of space for provocative contemporary exhibitions and performances. *Sat/Sun 10am–3pm, April–Oct Tue-Fri 9am–2pm and 7pm–9pm, Nov–Mar Wed–Fri 9am–2pm, Wed, Fri also 6pm–9pm | admission 3 euros | Odós Messolongíou 32 | www.cca.gr*

ODÓS VERNÁRDOU

Looking for a "food boulevard"? In the evening and at night, you need to head for the Odós Vernárdou, the most rus-

CITY **WHERE TO START!**
Platía Tésseron Mártiron:
Buses travelling from Iráklio and Chaniá stop at the *Platía Tésseron Mártiron* directly at the edge of the old town. South of this platía you will find a metered car park which offers the best parking spot – except Thursdays, which is when the large weekly market is held.

tic address. It has rows of typical Cretan *rakádika*, all serving Cretan delights in small portions – just the way the Cretans like them. Live music is played, and later at night the street itself becomes a party venue. And sometimes you can break with the style and start the evening with some classical music: there are occasional classical concert in the town's *Odeon*, which is in an old mosque on the Odós Vernárdou.

RIMÓNDI FOUNTAIN

The Venetian Rimondi Fountain is busiest during the day. The three stone lions' heads have been spouting water here since 1623. Four streets meet at the fountain, and anyone who is in Réthimno walks past at least once a day. It's the perfect spot to sit in a café and people-watch. *Platía Títu Peticháki*

VENETIAN HARBOUR ★

If you're worried about fish bones, opt for a tuna or swordfish steak instead. You have to eat in the old Venetian harbour at least once – ideally in the evening, when the building façades on the narrow, semi-circular quay look romantic instead of shabby, and the lighthouse dating back to Turkish times flashes a maritime greeting. Tiny colourful fishing boats are tied up in front of all the tables

and chairs outside the fish tavernas, leaving little space for people to walk past.

FOOD & DRINK

AVLÍ

The finest cuisine in all of Réthimno. Cretan and Mediterranean dishes are served here with the slogan "nostalgic with a modern touch". Guests can sit in a courtyard adorned with flowers and under the arches of a Venetian townhouse. The cellar is home to over 460 wines. *Daily from 7pm | Odós Xanthoudidou 22 | tel. 28 31 05 82 50 | www.avli.gr | Expensive*

INSIDER TIP KNOSSÓS

"Kráchtes" is what the Cretans call the waiters who talk to all the passers-by, attempting to lure them into their establishment. The English translation is, appropriately enough, "to lure".

There is only one single landlady in the Venetian harbour who doesn't do this: María, in the smallest of all the tavernas, the Knossós. Her elderly mother still does the cooking, while Maria herself runs the service with plenty of charm,

---

MARCO POLO HIGHLIGHTS

★ **Venetian harbour**
Crete's most beautiful harbour basin, lined with cafés and seafood tavernas
→ p. 49

★ **Arkádi Monastery**
This famous island monastery is a national shrine
→ p. 55

★ **Préveli Beach**
Two monasteries, a canyon and a dream of a beach – all very close together → p. 57

and her brother provides the entertainment with much clowning and plenty of music. The fish is served with frills or fuss – from the grill, with oil and lemon as the only dressing. *Daily from noon | Moderate*

OUSÍES ●

Of all the *rakádika* on the old town's "food boulevard", the Ousíes is the one with the most live Cretan music, namely the sounds of the lyre and laoúto. If you'd like to spend hours listening to it, you'll love the low price of the rakí *(2 euros/0.2 l)* and water pipe *(3.50 euros/ hour)*. *Summer daily 11am–2am, winter daily 5pm–2am | Odós Vernárdou 20 | Moderate*

LEMON TREE GARDEN

Would you like to eat like the Cretans but there are only two of you? This establishment specialises in couples. To enable you to experience as many Cretan specialities as possible during your meal, there are various mixed starter platters or entire three-course meals with a wide range of delights – with vegetarian and vegan options or request. All meals are served under lemon and pomegranate trees. *Daily from 11am | Odós Ethnikís Antistáseos 100 | Moderate*

SHOPPING

SHOPPING STREETS

The beautiful alley *Odós Arkadíu* in the old town is Réthimno's main shopping street. The locals also buy their shoes and clothes here. Souvenir shops can be found in Antistásseos, Súlion and Paleológou streets and the best Greek delicacies at *Avlí* at *Armanpatzóglou 40*.

LEISURE & SPORTS

The 16-km/9.9-mi sandy beach starts right in the town centre. And right at the start, *Ikarus (on the marina pier | tel. 69 70 09 96 23 | www.watersportikarus. com)* offers all kinds of water sports: jet skiing and water skiing, parasailing and kite surfing, banana rides and – for the slightly more cautious – even pedalos. Mountain biking needs are met by *Olympic Bike* (see p. 120) on the beach promenade to the east of the town, while guided walks are provided by *Happy Walker* (see p. 120).

ENTERTAINMENT

Where and when do things really get going? Well, first up before midnight at the *rakádika* in the Odós Vernárdou or the fabulously styled cocktail bars between the Venetian harbour and the marina. After midnight, the scene moves to the clubs on the short alleys right behind the Venetian harbour and the part of the Odós Salamínos near the marina.

ASTÉRIA ●

Open air cinema and bar underneath the Venetian fortress walls. At last you'll be able to hear Brad Pitt, Angelina Jolie and other celebrities in their original language. But under the fabulous Cretan starry sky, even the biggest Hollywood stars are bound to shrink to the size of starlets. *Admission 7 euros | Odós Melisínu/Odós Smírnis*

CUL DE SAC

The hotspot for warming up, right by the Rimondi Fountain. Also a good spot for asking locals where the action will be tonight. *Platía Titu Peticháki 5–9 | www. culdesac.gr*

DOME CLUB

One of the smaller discos in the town, which has the advantage that it looks full quicker. Resident and guest DJs constantly provide new sounds. *Odós Salamínos*

LIVINGROOM

The trendy bar on the promenade serves everything the young Greek heart desires, from Greek coffee to French champagne as well as 18 different Greek wines per glass and tasty ice cream sundaes. In typical Cretan fashion, guests receive a thirst quenching glass of water before they order. *Odós Eleftheríou Venizélou 5 | www.livingroom.gr*

METROPOLIS

The disco classic with lots of parties. Mainstream is popular. *Odós Neárchou 15 | in the Venetian harbour*

WHERE TO STAY

AQUILA RITHÝMNA BEACH

Do you like big hotel complexes? Then this is the place for you. There is a choice between hotel rooms and bungalows. Sea and fresh water pools, and even an indoor pool await you, plus a spa, water sports station and live music in the bar in the evenings. The (inexpensive) public bus into town stops right at the main entrance. *520 rooms | Ádele | tel. 28 31 07 10 02 | www.aquilahotels.com | Expensive*

Adaptable: in the evening, the Odós Vernárdo becomes a food boulevard first, and then it's party central!

CASA MAISTRA ⭒

If you're looking for somewhere to stay in the old town, the Casa Maistra offers modern furnished apartments in a historic 19th century building. You'll have plenty of space, because the holiday apartments all measure between 650–850 ft² over two floors. Plus you'll love the wonderful sea views and excellent value for money. It's only 10 minutes to the beach. *3 apartments | Odós Arkadíou 149 | tel. 28 31 03 05 70 | www.casamaistra.com | Expensive*

FORTÉZZA

This establishment (it also has a pool) blends harmoniously with the old town

Kite surfing at Rethimno beach: the stronger the wind, the more challenging the enjoyment

below the Fortézza, yet is situated in the middle of things. Ideal for tourists travelling with rental cars for stop-over accommodation, due to their free private car park. *54 rooms | Odós Melisínu 16 | tel. 28 31 05 55 55 | www.fortezza.gr | Moderate*

INSIDER TIP ▶ OLGA'S PENSION

Lovely old-fashioned guest house in the old town, somewhat chaotic, proprietor speaks good English, beautiful roof garden. A quaint meeting place for travellers! *8 rooms | tel. 28 31 05 32 06 | Odós Soulioú 57 | Budget*

PALAZZO VECCHIO

Hotel in a Venetian palace dating from the 15th century. A small pool in the courtyard and a terrace with deckchairs and umbrellas on the roof. *25 apartments | Odós Melissínou/Platía Iróon Politechníu | tel. 28 31 03 53 51 | www. palazzovecchio.gr | Expensive*

INFORMATION

TOURIST INFORMATION
Prokiméa Elefthérios Venizélou | tel. 28 31 02 91 48 | www.rethymnon.gr

WHERE TO GO

AGÍA GALÍNI (146 B4) (*Ø* H5)
If you are anything but shy, then you'll feel completely at home in this village, which has the pretty name of "Holy Tranquillity". The densely built centre stretches from the harbour up a narrow valley that has most of the hotels and guesthouses on its slopes. The actual centre is formed by three vertical and two horizontal streets full of shops, bars and cafés. Most of the tavernas reach up

several floors right next to the harbour square, their roof gardens and terraces sparkling with lights in the evenings between the sky and the sea. All of life plays on an area measuring about 100 x 200 m/330 x 660 ft, so you'll keep meeting the same people. A good place for rendezvous is the modern memorial to the mythical aviators Daedalus' and Icarus on the terrace above the harbour. There's swimming on a long, narrow beach 200 m/660 ft to the north of the harbour. and throughout the day there are several boats out to the beaches in the area and as far as *Préveli Beach* (see p. 57). You'll be a little off the beaten tracks but extremely comfortable in the five rooms and six studios of the *Romantika Apartments (tel. 28 32 09 13 88 | www.agia-galini.com | Moderate)*, which also has an extremely good street taverna. Delicious Cretan food is served at *Ílios (Moderate)* near the bus stop. *55 km/34.2 mi*

ARGIROÚPOLI (144 C4) (*𝄪 F4*)

Mountain villages don't have to be boring – you can easily spend a whole day in this one. It's best to start in the village church with its filigree clock tower. Right next door, a sign draws your attention to some old stone blocks: building remains of the antique town of Lappa, which once stood here. Diagonally opposite is the way in to the old Venetian village. The archway is the first thing that will leave you speechless: there are displays of all kinds of ⊛ INSIDER TIP hand creams, gels and lotions made from avocados, which have been grown in the region since the 1990s, that you can buy. You can get a free map of the town in the shop. The INSIDER TIP nameless kafenío is a nice place to drink a coffee or avocado juice and eat avocado and shrimps. An approximately 30-minute tour of the village takes you to a lovely Roman floor mosaic and the photogenic little chapel of *Agía Paraskeví*. The lid of an antique child's sarcophagus is also the step down to the churchyard. Then there's a little unspoilt countryside, sprinkled with ancient graves. Follow the signs on the little road to Káto Póros 400 m/1300 ft further, and then to the "Holly 5 Virgins". These little rock graves are about 2000 years old, and you can walk over some of them. For lunch, trout and sturgeon, freshly caught in the strong springs, await you in the tavernas. To dine in an historic ambience, head for *Au Vieux Moulin (daily from 11am | Moderate)*, in and around an old water mill. On the way back via Réthimno, you can stop at the modern shop, which makes innovative use of another traditional natural product: at the *Creta Carob Shop (www.cretacarob.com)*, you will find all sorts of natural products made from carob, from syrup to tea, coffee and cocoa. *21 km/13.1 mi*

Arkádi Monastery where silence and peace reign today – once the scene of bloody battles

ARMÉNI (145 D4) (*(Ø) F3*)

Crete's prettiest cemetery is situated in a forest of kermes and Vallonea oaks. Over the past 50 years, archaeologists have excavated more than 230 tombs. The deceased were buried there about 3300 years ago. They are all of different sizes, and you can enter many of them. It's not at all spooky; in fact, it actually makes you want to have a picnic in the countryside. *Apr–Oct Tue–Sun 10am–6pm, Nov–Mar Tue–Sun 8am–3pm | admission 3 euros. 6 km/3.7 mi*

ASÓMATOS (145 D5) (*(Ø) F4*)

The village priest Michális Georgioulákis (1921–2008) always did everything differently and as such his village museum INSIDER TIP *Oriseum (daily 10am–5pm | admission 3.50 euros)* is quite unique. On display is everything that he has collected from surrounding villages, bought at flea markets or inherited over the past 60 years. *30 km/18.6 mi*

ELÉFTHERNA (146 B2) (*(Ø) H3*)

Since the Minoans were immigrants from Asia rather than Greek, the excavations at Eléftherna are extremely important to today's Cretans. Genuine Hellenes lived here two to three thousand years ago, something that is also emphasised in the state-of-the-art *Museum (Tue–Sun 10am–6pm | admission 4 euros)*, which only opened in 2016. This is also confirmed by the *three archaeological sites* that you can explore on a half-day hike from here. However, before heading there, check at the museum whether they are still accessible or have been closed due to a lack of funds. *22 km/13.7 mi*

victims are now on display in glass cabinets in the *Mausoleum* opposite the entrance to the monastery. Flowers are still placed on an altar in the now roofless powder magazine, while the story of Arkádis is told in more detail in the monastery *Museum (May, Sep, Oct daily 9am–7pm, Jun–Aug daily 9am–8pm, otherwise daily 9am–5pm | admission 2.50 euros)*. *23 km/14.3 mi*

MARGARÍTES ● (146 B2) (*∅ H3*)

Are you still looking for a few souvenirs? You'll find an excellent selection in Margarítes. More than 20 ceramicists work here in studios along the village street, producing art and kitsch, useful things or simply pretty things on their wheels. In the midst of them all, landlady Eléni prepares her legendary moussaká fresh every morning at *Gianousákis (daily from 10am | Budget)*. *27 km/16.8 mi*

MELIDÓNI (146 B1) (*∅ H3*)

Now you have to be brave. That's because the latest attraction in this pretty, old village is ● *Reptisland (summer daily 8am–8pm, winter daily 9am–3pm | admission 3 euros | next to the petrol station at the north entrance to the village)* with scorpions, tarantulas, frogs, lizards and giant snakes from all over the world. The Papakostánti brothers, whose animals they are, will be pleased to place the frog on your hand for you to waken with a kiss – or, if you prefer, wrap a 5 m/16.4 ft long python around your shoulders. If you would then like to relax, you can drive up to the *Melidóni stalactite cave (daily 8am until sunset | admission 4 euros)*, which is only 2 km/1.2 mi away. The bones and skulls on the altar that commemorate a Turkish massacre in 1835 will hardly alarm you now. Nor will the black men you might see on the side of the road into the neighbouring

ARKÁDI MONASTERY ★
(145 F4) (*∅ G4*)

Can mass suicide be a heroic deed? Crete's clear answer to that is "yes". Which is why the monastery on an isolated high plain has been declared a national shrine of the island. In 1866, Cretan insurgents entrenched themselves here, together with their wives and children, against approaching Turkish troops. When, after a two-days siege in the monastery, the Turks broke into the monastery, the insurgents gathered in the powder magazine and blew themselves up rather than face rape and enslavement. Over 900 Christians died. The story of this "heroic" suicide quickly spread throughout the world, and ultimately led to Crete finally being annexed to the Greek motherland in 1913. The bones and skulls of numerous

It's easy to stroll to the villages of Sellía and Mýrthios from Plakiás

village of Agía: they are charcoal burners, who still produce charcoal the traditional way in piles under the open sky. If you would like to take something with you to remind you of this special place, go to the modern ● INSIDER TIP ▶ *Olive oil factory Paráskákis (open daily | admission free)* on the road to Pérama. After a guided tour, you can then buy the olive oil at Ioánna Paraskáki. *31 km/19.3 mi*

PLAKIÁS (145 D5) (⌖ F4)

Do you have no objections to all-inclusive holidays, but prefer somewhere that is for individualists? Then Plakiás

is the answer. The sandy beach is over 800 m/2600 ft long, and widens to the west into a dune landscape – where you can also obtain an all-over tan. Almost all of the bars and tavernas are right beside the water, and there are daily boat trips out from the tiny harbour to *Préveli Beach* (see p. 57). (see p. 57) Signposted hiking trails lead through olive groves and past old water mills and up into the mountain villages *Mýrthios* and *Sellía*, where you will also find craft shops as well as good tavernas. There is affordable jewellery in Mýrthios from Josíf Petrákis at the *Líthos Nature Collection*, and in Selliá from Jánnis and Angelika at the *Ikaros*. *Carola Poppinga* from East Friesland makes guardian angels from alpaca wire in Selliá, while *Jánnis Méxis* and *Pinélopi Kostogiánni* shape fabulous items out of wood and modelling clay in Mýrthios. The *Anso* travel agency organises guided tours and mountain bike rides. A lovely place to stay is near the dunes at the *Hotel Plakias Bay (tel. 28 32 03 12 15 | www.plakiasbay.com | Moderate)*, which has an excellent taverna. *40 km/24.9 mi*

POTAMÓN RESERVOIR
(145 E4) (⌖ G4)

Sifis is gone! For nine months in 2014/15, the 2-m/6.6-ft crocodile swam in Crete's newest reservoir. No one knew where it had come from, but then it was found starved, floating on the water. It is still talked about at the *Café Potamon (daily from 10am | Budget)* on the 310-m/1000-ft long dam wall, and the creature's plastic brother hangs from the ceiling. Something wonderful awaits you at *Ágios Antónios gorge* in the nearby village of Pátsos, starting at the large, generously signposted forest taverna *Drymos (daily from 10am | Budget)*, where lovers of hearty meat dishes find plenty of (affordable) dishes, as do vegetarians with a taste for the unusual. Just a five-minute walk later, you'll be in the gorge gazing in at the *tiny cave chapel of St Antónios* with the most curious forms of the orthodox belief in miracles: notes with prayers have been slipped into cracks in the rocks; romper suits hang inside the church, and crutches have been placed in the corners. *21 km/13.1 mi*

PRÉVELI ⭐ (145 D–E6) (*ⅆ F5*)

You can spend an entire day of your holiday at Préveli. There is a terrific beach, a lovely taverna, an old bridge, two monasteries and a canyon full of palm trees – short walk included. Coming from the main road, after 2 km/1.2 mi you first cross a photogenic bridge with a lovely arch that farmers used to cross with their donkeys. By the rushing mountain stream below is a good *taverna (daily from 10am | Budget)* with ducks outside that you can feed. A further 600 m/2000 ft below the road are the accessible ruins of the *Káto Préveli Monastery*. The road ends 3.2 km/2 mi further at the *Piso Préveli Monastery (25 March–May daily 9am–7pm, June–Oct Mon–Sat 9am–1.30pm and 3.30pm–7pm, Sun 9am–7pm | admission 2.50 euros)*. In 1941, the monks hid British soldiers until they could be picked up by submarines.

Between Káto and Píso Préveli, a cul-de-sac branches off towards the coast, and ends at a car park *(2 euros/day)*. A steep footpath takes you from there down to the Préveli stream in about 30 minutes. A river with cold water flows across the beach (about 200 m/660 ft long) into the sea from the Kourtaliátiko Gorge, a narrow canyon overgrown by palm trees. You might be able to manage the walk towards the source as far as the taverna with the ducks. You will have to clamber over rapids and rocks, wade through knee high or chest high water and at certain places you even have to swim. *37 km/23 mi*

SPÍLI (145 E5) (*ⅆ G4*)

Crete's must-do programme: on the drive between the north and south coasts, stop at the large, old mountain village of Spíli. Have coffee on the shady Platía with its Venetian fountain with water bubbling forcefully from numerous lions' heads –and then drive on. *30 km/18.6 mi*

FOR BOOKWORMS AND FILM BUFFS

Alexis Sorbas – A Cretan classic (both book and film) written by Níkos Kazantzákis and directed by Michael Cacoyannis in 1964 with Anthony Quinn, Alan Bates and Irene Pappas in the lead roles still radiates a strong feeling of *Cretan joie de vie*.

The Island – This historical novel by award-winning author Victoria Hislop is set on the former leper colony of Spinalónga, an island off the Cretan coast.

He Who Must Die – A 1956 film directed by Jules Dassin based on the novel *Christ Recrucified* by Níkos Kazantzákis and filmed mainly in Krítsa. It starred Melina Mercouri and Gert Fröbe.

IRÁKLIO

Landed safely? Every year, more than 6 million passengers land at Iráklio (Heraklion) airport, and more than one-third of all Cretans live in the greater area of the island's capital.

Large hotels focus on the northern coat between Heraklion and Mália, but here there is absolutely no talk of the kind of mass tourism that is found on the coasts of other countries. On the southern coast, even individualists will feel completely at home, and in between are vineyards, the fertile Messará Plain, and two wild mountain ranges. Excursions into the Minoan palace towns of Festós and Knossós go back 3500 years, where five-storey houses were nothing new even then. In fact, this was the home of Europe's first advanced civilisation.

IRÁKLIO

MAP INSIDE BACK COVER
(147 E–F2) *(⌀ K–L3)* **Have no fear! From a distance, Iráklio (pop. almost 200,000) may look like a Moloch, but at the centre the city is pretty, clearly laid out and, above all, bursting with urban life. By day and night.**

Road traffic has been brought well under control in recent years; traffic lights have been removed and many passenger precincts created. Which means there is now even more room for tavernas and street cafés. As a shopping metropolis, Iráklio is unbeaten on the island – and its museums are among the most important in Greece.

Photo: Morosíni fountain on Iráklio's Platía Venizélou

The heartbeat of the island: the ancient centre of the Minoan world has evolved into the centre of Mediterranean holiday life

🏙 WHERE TO START?

Venetian harbour: to avoid the problem of finding parking in Iráklio, it is best to go there by bus. If you arrive by car, you can park along the shore at the commercial port (partly free), then walk in a westerly direction for about 5–15 minutes to the Venetian harbour on the edge of the old town.

SIGHTSEEING

ÁGIOS MÁRKOS CHURCH

The oldest Venetian church built in 1239 (close to the Morosini Fountain) today hosts concerts and exhibitions. The monolithic pillars of the basilica date back to ancient times. *Opening times differ | admission free | Odós 25 Avgústu*

ÁGIOS MINÁS CHURCH

Do you like looking through colourful picture books? The cathedral of Iráklio,

Flood of recent images: ceiling paintings in Iráklio's Ágios Cathedral

about 150 years old, is one – a picture book that up to 8000 people can read at the same time. Cupolas, arches and walls are completely covered in paintings of numerous biblical stories. Turn it into a search game, and try to find (at the very least) the story of the Birth of Jesus and his crucifixion. Any others that you find will certainly earn you additional points in heaven! *Usually open during the day / admission free / Platía Agía Ekaterínis*

ÁGIOS TÍTOS CHURCH

Holy hoo-ha? Many Cretans would beg to differ. They believe that the skull in the silver reliquary in the side chapel on the left really is that of St Titus, the island's first bishop almost 2000 years ago. *Daily 7am–noon and 5pm–8pm / admission free / Odós 25 Avgústu*

ARCHAEOLOGICAL MUSEUM ⭐

If not here, then where? The two-storey museum contains more finds from Minoan times than all of the other museums in the world combined. And as well as noble art, it also contains numerous items that speak to us of everyday life here – about 3500 years ago. On display are Minoan house facades made from tiles, a board game, clay model ships and houses, jewellery and a number of seals. One of the most valuable pieces is a vessel in the shape of a bull's head carved from soapstone with rock crystal eyes and a mother of pearl mouth and a rhyton, a drinking and alms vessel made of shimmering rock crystal.

The 3500-year old Phaistos disc is particularly fascinating. It is covered on both sides with a spiral of 241 hieroglyphics stamped into the clay, the meaning of which has never been conclusively explained. The wall murals in the Palace of Knossós and the Minoan villas are staggeringly beautiful – they look like prehistoric photo wallpaper. *April–Oct daily 8am–8pm, Nov–March Mon 11am–5pm, Tue–Sun 8am–3pm | admission 10 euros (Nov–March 5 euros), combined ticket with Knossós 16 euros (8 euros) | Platía Eleftherías/Odós Xanthudínu*

EARTHQUAKE SIMULATOR ●

What does it feel like when the earth quakes? That is something that no one would really want to experience, but in the simulator of the Museum of Natural History it's both interesting and perfectly safe. In a replica of an old classroom, earthquakes of various forces give you a good shaking every half-hour. *Mon–Fri 9am–9pm, Sat/Sun 10am–9pm | admission 9 euros | Leof. Sof. Venizélou | www.nhmc.uoc.gr*

HISTORICAL MUSEUM

What did Iráklio look like 400 years ago? A large wooden model shows it clearly at a scale of 1:500. Also interesting: medieval hand grenades made of glass and ceramic, Cretan folk costumes and art, an office of the Sorbás author Níkos Kazantzákis. And for art-lovers, two small paintings by El Greco. *Mon–Sat 9am–5pm, winter until 3.30pm | admission 5 euros | Odós Lysimachou Kalokerinou 7 | www.historical-museum.gr*

KÚLES FORTRESS ⚜

This will get your blood flowing. First you climb under the dark arches of the Venetian harbour fort and up onto the roof to look over the old town to the Cretan mountains. Then you can join the joggers running a circuit along the approx. 1 km/0.6 mi pier. *Tue–Sun 8am–3pm | admission 3 euros | the pier of the fishing harbour*

MOROSÍNI FOUNTAIN

Arranging somewhere to meet? The Venetian "lion" fountain is the general meeting place of the city. It's where all the main day- and night-time streets come together: the wide pedestrian street is 25is Avgústou, the main shopping streets Dédalu, 1866 and Kalokerinú, and the nightlife areas Handakós and Platía Korái. The fountain square itself is perfect for a gyros in the hand or a bugátsa in a café – with the people from all over the world as a source of constant entertainment. *Platía Venizélou*

MUSEUM OF CHRISTIAN ART

Icons are not for everyone, but for those who do appreciate them, here are six masterpieces by Michaíl Damaskinós, the most important representative of the Cretan style of holy art in the 16th century. *Apr–Oct daily 9.30am–7.30pm, daily Nov–Mar 9.30am–6pm | admission 4 euros | Platía Ekaterínis*

MARCO POLO HIGHLIGHTS

★ **Archaeological Museum**
The treasures of Minoan Crete → p. 60

★ **Knossós**
Captivating ruins of archaeology's „Disneyland" → p. 66

★ **Mátala**
Hippie caves, old fishing village, sandy beaches – easy to get lost in your memories → p. 68

★ **Festós**
A Minoan palace with a fantastic view → p. 70

ODÓS 1866

Although the 200-m/660-ft street is no longer a traditional market for locals, there's still plenty going on. It's an excellent place to shop for culinary souvenirs, to pop into rather old-fashioned tavernas and cafenía or modern bistros and coffee shops. The best place to sit is on the eastern end of the street beside the Venetian Bembo fountain, which is adorned by a headless antique statue.

FOOD & DRINK

INSIDER TIP ▶ KIRKOR AND FYLLO...SOPHIES

Fancy something sweet? These two cafés serve *bougátsa*, a type of semolina pudding with phyllo pastry, dusted with lots of icing sugar. A savoury version is the *bougátsa tirí* made with a sheeps' cheese filling. *Daily from 6am | Morosini Fountain | Budget*

PÁNTHEON

This market taverna has remained delightfully old-fashioned. The selection of cooked, fried and baked foods is vast, and guests choose the fish or steak for their meals themselves from the fridge. Everything is done quickly, even though afterwards you'd like to sit for a while, nursing a retsína. *Mon–Sat from 8pm | Odós Theodosáki/Odós 1866 | Budget*

TOU TERZÁKI

Help wanted! Because Cretans like to spend a long time discussing what to eat with everyone else at the table, an old custom is coming back into fashion: the waiter presents the guests with a list instead of a menu, and they then put a cross by all the things they'd like to eat. There are plenty of unusual dishes as well as all the usuals – why not try Cretan snails? *Daily from 11am, Sun in winter from 6pm | Odós Marinélli 17 | Moderate*

SHOPPING

BSB FASHION

Female, aged between 18 and 34? Then this is the place for you! BSB is one of the biggest fashion companies in Greece, and is currently expanding worldwide and in the web. From denim to festive, metallic to the office – at last there are plenty of different choices from what you normally find at home! *Odós Idís 26–28 | www.bsbfashion.com*

BYZANTINE HERITAGE

You'll find silver-plated fashion jewellery from as little as 7 euros in this shop on the market street, and almost nothing over 50 euros. What is lovely about it: you can tell by the designs that this charming gift was made in Greece. *Odós 1866 | byzantine-heritage.com*

TSAKÍRIS MÁLLAS

Art for the feet: the ladies of Crete love going out in the most progressive shoes, sandals and boots made by Greek shoe artists – but there's also plenty on offer for the more conservative, for men and for children, all usually at reasonable prices. *Odós Dédalu 30–32 | tsakiris mallas.gr*

BEACHES

Too hot in the city? *Public bus services (astiko-irakleiou.gr)* will take you to the nearby beaches for very little money: line 6 takes you from the bus station at the harbour to the mile-long sandy beach at Ammoudára, line 7 from the Platía Eleftherías outside the Archaeological Museum to the sandy beach at Amnissós.

ENTERTAINMENT

In the evenings young Iráklion people meet in the bars and music cafés at ● *Platía Korái* while a more alternative public frequent the little bars in the *Odós Chandakós*. Dance clubs open around midnight in *Odós Epimenídu* and at the western edge of the old town at the coastal road *S. Venizélu*.

BLOW UP

More of a pub with music than a bar, more alternative than mainstream. Lots of students. DJs every evening, sometimes soul, blues and funk live. In short: it's a good place to talk to people as well. Daily from 8pm | *15 Odós Psaromilíngon*

ENVY

Disco like at home? That would be the Envy Club, a firm fixture in the city's young nightlife. There's often live Greek rock music in summer, when you'll have to pay for admission *(20 euros including 1 drink)*. Daily from 11pm | *Leof. Sof. Venizélou | Tálos Centre*

MILOS STAGE

Critics describe the live Greek music that is played here at weekends and attracts up to 300 fans as *skiládika* – like howling dogs with something to celebrate. This is the place to go if you would like to see Cretans relaxed and dancing Greek dances. The place really starts buzzing at 1am. *Fri/Sat from 11.30pm | Odós Lachaná/Mitsotáki | tel. for bookings 69 36 78 77 10*

TITA PRIKI

Around midnight this usually quite normal bar usually turns into party central for singles. Admission is free, the music Greek and international. *Daily from noon | Odós Mirabélu 8*

So beautifully traditional that you'll be happy to stay a little longer: Pántheon market taverna

WETS & DRYS SPEAKEASY BAR

Prohibition on Crete? Unimaginable. Alcohol can flow freely here. But then again, thought a few Cretans, perhaps a little bit of prohibition is not a bad thing. And brought the idea of the American "speakeasy" bar back to life, those secret places where people would hit the alcohol in a big way despite the ban. You need a four-digit code to get in, but the bouncer will be pleased to share it with you. Mainly cocktails and other elegant drinks are served on the two floors on the inside, and often there are guest bartenders with ideas for brand new cocktails. The music is on the old-fashioned side, the audience mostly aged between 30 and 50. *Daily 7.20pm-5am | Odós Korái 7*

WHERE TO STAY

CANDIA SUITES
Small, but at excellent prices! Opened in 2016, the five studios and apartments are ultra-chic and of entirely different sizes. The fishing harbour and bus station are three minutes away, and it even has private parking (*10 euros/day*). *Odós Lachaná 13–15 | tel. 69 44 58 25 09 | www.candiasuites.gr | Budget–Moderate*

LENA
Would you rather spend your money on something else? Then stay at this simple, somewhat old-fashioned hotel instead. The atmosphere is warm and friendly, the location right in the centre. *16 rooms | Odós Lachaná 10 | tel. 28 10 22 32 80 | www.lena-hotel.gr | Budget*

OLIVE GREEN ⊛
The DNA of this hotel: eco and smart. Opened in 2016, much is digital: you can even check in and out using the smartphone app. The rooms are at least 215 ft² big, and all have a balcony or terrace. The bathrooms also have a walk-in rainforest shower. *48 rooms | Odós Idomenéos 22 | tel. 28 10 24 03 50 | www.olivegreenhotel. com | Moderate*

INFORMATION

TOURIST INFORMATION
Near the Morosíni fountain | tel. 28 13 40 97 77

WHERE TO GO

ANÓGIA (146 C2) (*ጠ J4*)
Where does the heart of "real Crete" beat? Most locals will tell you: in Anógia! And in three ways: they mostly listen to the traditional Cretan music of the Xyloúris family, widely regarded as the musical royal family of the island and hailing from Anógia. The family's main home in the lower Platía of the village is now a *museum (open during the day | admission free)*. In the minds of the Cre-

LOW BUDGET

For good, low-budget food 24/7, the grill bars at Iráklio's *Platía Kallergón* close to the Morosíni fountain are always a good place to head for. A portion of gyros with salad and roasted potatoes will cost you around just 3 euros.

A city bus leaves every 5 minutes from the Iráklio airport for the city centre and the long distance bus terminal. Tickets for 1.40 euros can be bought from the ticket window at the bus stop.

Not just a picture book village, but for the Cretans the island's most symbolic place: Anógia

tans, Anógia is the symbol of the resistance to the German occupiers in WWII – in 1944, they burnt the town down as punishment for the embarrassing abduction of their General Heinrich Kreipe to Egypt, and shot all the men they could find in the village. This is commemorated in a plaque and memorial near the town hall in the upper part of the village. Scenes of the occupation and resistance were also the main themes of the naïve village painter, whose work can be seen in the *Museum of Alkiwíades Skulás Grílios (key at the Kafeníon Skulás | admission free)* near the lower village square. However, one of the main reasons Anógia is considered the "heart of Creta" is also because it is home to the island's biggest flocks of sheep and goats. Over 100,000 animals provide milk, cheese and meat. and they graze mainly on the common land of the uninhabited ● *Nída Plateau* at the foot of the Psilorítis, which is reached by a 21 km/13.1 mi road. Many Cretans come to the tavernas of Anógia

for their meat at the weekends in particular. Very good: *Gagáris (daily from 10am | Moderate)* in the upper part of the village on the one-way street down. *43 km/26.7 mi*

CHERSÓNISOS (148 B–C2) (*ℳ M3*)

This is where it's at! *Liménas Chersónisou* is the international party metropolis on the island. The traffic-free beach promenade is almost 2 km/1.2 mi long with lots of tavernas, café bars, pubs and music clubs. About 200 m/660 ft from the beach is the equally long main street with hundreds of shops and more pubs and restaurants. It's never boring here, which is why people are also happy to accept that in the town itself, there is too little beach for too many people. Instead, they use the many hotel pools or the *Star Beach Club (admission free)* on the northern outskirts of the town with its water slides and party sounds that start in the morning. Still, when you want to escape from the noise and bustle, then head to the mountainside villages of *Koutou-loufári* and *Piskopianó, which are about 20 minutes away*. With their narrow streets and natural brick buildings, they are every bit as idyllic as you probably expected Crete to be. You can easily spend an evening in the elegant cocktail bars. A good "Cretan village evening" *(Mon from approx. 8pm | Moderate)* with music and folk dancing is also organised by the innkeepers at the tavernas on the Platía of the village of *Chersónisos*, for which Liménas Chersónisou was until 50 years ago merely a poor boat mooring. If you haven't booked at Chersónisos, don't even bother going there – unless you want to learn a lot about life on Crete before the tourists came. You'll learn so much from the exhibits in the private Open-air museum *Lychnostátis (Sun–Fri 9am–2pm | admission 5 euros)* on the eastern outskirts of the town – in an extremely entertaining way. *26 km/15.2 mi*

FÓDELE (147 D1) (*𝄞 J3*)

Interested in art? In this village in between orange and olive groves the painter Doménikos Theotokópulos was born in 1541. He later became known worldwide as El Greco. The home in which he was born *(May–Sept daily 9am–7pm, April–Nov daily 8.30am–3pm | admission 2.50 euros)* has been wonderfully reconstructed. A lovely *kafenío* and a church from the 10th century are in front of it. The church has a mosaic depicting fishermen at work. *29 km/18 mi*

KNOSSÓS (147 F2) (*𝄞 L4*)

The no. 1 of the island's top sights. 3500 years ago, the so-called "palace" of ★ Knossós was already a major town with a population of perhaps 80,000. At the time, we were still living in caves, but here some people even lived in four-storey houses with sewage systems, paved roads and squares. Pretty frescoes adorned the walls, and works of art of a unique elegance were created in workshops, while the people kept stores of provisions in vast jugs in storage rooms. And although the people of Knossós used a form of writing, they did so mainly for recording the dates of their stores and provisions; they passed nothing of themselves and their history on to us.

The Englishman Sir Arthur Evans only unearthed the settlement in the first quarter of the last century – and then rebuilt it in sections which is why, unlike in other places, you can see more than just a few layouts and walls. Columns and pillars support many a roof, and murals adorn the walls. In fact, your own imagination will be helped to let pre-historic life come to life again. Also of help are the postcards with the coloured reconstruction drawing of the whole complex, which you can buy near the cash desk.

The "palace" was without doubt a multi-purpose building. Religious ceremonies played a large part. In festivals, long processions progressed through long corridors, as can be seen in the frescoes on the wall of the west corridor at the beginning of a tour. They were heading for the large central courtyard. Adjoining it to the west are a number of dark halls, such as the pillar crypts, which imitate cave sanctuaries. Sir Arthur even found a kind of throne in one room. Perhaps it was left unoccupied for a deity, or perhaps it was used by a priestess. He even assumed it might have been reserved for the legendary king. He also believed he had found, in the former four-storey building on the eastern side of the central courtyard, the rooms of the king and queen, both of which had a water closet, although there is some doubt about this today. It is more likely to have been a building with luxury apartments. *Apr–Oct daily*

8am–8pm, Nov–Mar 8am–3pm | admission 15 euros, combi-ticket with Archaeological Museum Iráklio 16 euros | From Iráklio the city bus no. 2 leaves from the bus station at the harbour and from the bus stop in front of house number 62 in Odos 1821, every 20 minutes to Knossós, which is only 5 km/3.1 mi away.

MÁLIA (148 C2) (*ᗰ M–N4*)

Prince Harry would like, The Queen less so: this expansive holiday resort is usually firmly in the hands of young British visitors. Nowhere else are the screens in the sports bars bigger, the quads more numerous on the streets, the tattoo studios open longer at night. Shots and beer flow freely – and yet potatoes still thrive in the deep-red fields among all the bars, clubs and hotels. The fine sandy beach is lovely and wide, and miles long. If you stay at one of the better hotels, you'll hardly notice all the noise and bustle. And if you find yourself wanting to see the more traditional Crete, stroll through old Mália on the other side of the main road, where the taverna *Kalesma (daily from 6.30pm | Odós Omirú 8 | Expensive)* still serves traditional Cretan cuisine. Lovers of ancient ruins never miss the Minoan *Palace of Mália (Tue–Sun 8am–3pm | admission 6 euros)* on the eastern edge of the town. 3500 years ago, it was the third-biggest one on Crete. *37 km/23 mi*

TÍLISSOS (147 D2) (*ᗰ K4*)

Would you like a romantic breather? Then head for the little-visited excavations of three Minoan country houses on the edge of the village today. The old pine trees will provide you and the 3500-year-old walls with plenty of shade.

Flowering capers climb up them in the early summer. Cicadas will perform a

Start with the palace of Knossós if you want to get to know Minoan culture

private concert for you as you snooze in the grass. And once again, you'll be amazed by the exceptionally highly-developed architecture of the Minoans: water pipes lead to the former two-storey buildings, feeding a cistern. Vast, lavishly decorated storage containers are dotted about, some of them still almost intact. How delicious would the wine have been, sipped here with the views of the green hills of Crete! *Daily from 9am–4pm | admission 2 euros. 15 km/9.3 mi*

ZONIANÁ (146 C2) (*ⓜ J4*)

The mountain village is considered the centre of Crete's hemp cultivation, which frequently leads to police raids. But if you don't act like a secret policeman or photo reporter, you'll find the village as harmless and peaceful as all the others. If perhaps a little poorer. There's also something to see: on the outskirts of the village is the 550-m/1800-ft long ● *Sventóni stalactite cave (Apr–Oct daily from 10.30am–5pm,*

Nov–Mar only Sat/Sun 10.30am–2.30pm | admission 4 euros | www.zoniana.gr), and directly on the Platía the *Waxworks museum Potamiós (summer daily 10am–7pm, winter 10am–5.30pm | admission 2.50 euros)* with reproductions à la Madame Tussaud of important events in the history of Crete, from Minos to today. *43 km/26.7 mi*

MÁTALA

(146 B5) (*ⓜ H6*) Today is life. Tomorrow never comes! That was and is the motto of the former fishing village of ★ Mátala on the south coast.

During the Vietnam war, Mátala made a name for itself as a stronghold for hippies. Today the annual Mátala Festival, which takes place around Whitsun, reawakens old memories. During the rest of the summer, hippie flair combines with day visitors and the usual holiday-makers. Now, the curious scramble around the caves

The hippie caves in the long rock of Mátala are empty, but the bay is still popular

in the rock wall on the north side of the bay that were once burial sites for the Romans and then, centuries later, homes for the flower children. In the few buildings and boat sheds on the south side of the old fishing settlement, people dine in rustic fish tavernas before enjoying the night in cool hammocks or tiny music clubs. Between the two shores is a wide sandy beach some 200 m/660 ft long, and behind that a short bazaar alley that is still a little like a north African souk. There are guesthouses in the town, while hotels for all-inclusive visitors are in the 2-km/1.2-mi valley beyond it.

FOOD & DRINK

AKUNA MATATA

The name is Swahili, and sums up the venue: no problems. Cool location on the water, psychedelic colours, 1970s atmosphere and music. Flower power times – almost is if you were there. Except that

back then, people didn't drink cocktails or eat finger food or scampi, and still made their own music. *Daily from 11am | old fishing quarter | Budget–Moderate*

MYSTICAL VIEW ☼

The view makes the difference: you sit high above Kómo here, overlooking the Psilorítis and watching the sun sink into the sea. It's almost mystical. The quality of the food is rather more normal. Signposted on the road to *Pitsídia, approx. 2.5 km/1.5 mi from Mátala | Moderate*

SHOPPING

AXEL GENTHNER

In the shop and studio of this gold- and silversmith who settled in Mátala long ago, you'll find the kind of jewellery that no one else is wearing. *Sun–Fri 1pm–7pm | main street, in the shopping area at the Hotel Zafiria*

BEACHES

KÓMO BEACH

Over 2 km/1.2 mi long and 40 m/131.2 ft wide. A taverna at the southern end, a small town right at the north. Otherwise just find sand that you don't have to have bathing trunks or a bikini for. Unfortunately, it's 3 km/1.9 mi from Mátala, but then – that's what mopeds are for.

MÁTALA BEACH

The beach for comfort-lovers, right in town. Full in summer, but relaxed. Hardly no recliners for hire, but people bring their own beach towels.

RED BEACH

The red shimmering beach for walkers, a 30-minute walk from the village. Almost as far from civilisation as in the old hippie days.

ENTERTAINMENT

PORT SIDE

DJs play until 5am, and occasionally there's live music right beside the sea. Breakfast is available from 8am – and in between, you can go for a swim. *Old fishing quarter*

WHERE TO STAY

DIMITRIS VILLA

Hippie flair is nice, but having a few home comforts is nicer. All 20 rooms here have satellite TV, fridges and safes, and the hotel also has a pool and bicycles for guests to use. It's 800 m/2600 ft to the beach. *In the hotel valley | tel. 28 92 04 50 02 | Budget*

MÁTALA VIEW

Close to the beach and right in the village? As you wish – the Androulákis family has 17 rooms and apartments waiting for you. *Guesthouse alley | tel. 28 92 04 51 14 | www.matala-apartments.com | Budget*

WHERE TO GO

FESTÓS ★ ☆ (146 C5) (*ⓜ J5*)

First Knossós, then Festós – that's the correct sequence for the two most significant Minoan palace towns on Crete. If you visit *Knossós* (see p. 66) first, you'll have a better idea of what Festós looked like 3500 years ago – today all that remains are a few foundation walls. Although they are in a delightful landscape on a hilly plateau with views of the Psilorítis and Asteroúsia mountains. Even if you'd rather save the admission fee, it's worth going to the ☆ INSIDER TIP terrace of the excavation café is probably the loveliest on the island, plus you'll have close views of the Minoan town.

However, if you are greatly interested in Minoan Crete, then drive another 2 km/1.2 mi to the excavation of the tiny Minoan palace at *Agía Triáda (Apr–Oct daily from 9.30am–4.30pm, otherwise Tue-Sun 9am-3pm | admission 4 euros)* in a shady little wood. *Apr–Oct daily from 8am-8pm, otherwise daily from 8am-5pm | admission 8 euros. 10 km/6.2 mi*

GÓRTIS (147 D5) (*ⓜ J5*)

Duty first … the ruins of the island's Roman capital are on both sides of the road. On the north, they are fenced in and you have to pay to get in *(Apr–Oct daily from 8am-8pm, otherwise 8am–3pm | admission 6 euros)*. See the remains of the towering walls of the *Títus Basilica, which dates back to the 6th century BC, and the Odéon*, a small Roman theatre for music and pantomime. Now under cover and behind bars are twelve of what were once 20 tablets of rules, carved around 500 BC. You'll learn a lot about the civil and criminal law of the time from these 42 stone blocks with 17,000 letters. Behind them is a meadow with an ancient olive tree, under which Zeus, the father of the gods, allegedly fathered Minos with Europa.

There are many more olive trees on the other side of the road (no admission) to the ● *remains* of countless Roman buildings, including an *amphitheatre*, the *Governor's palace* and a *thermal spa*. Very few visitors, so you can enjoy Antiquity in delightful peace and solitude. *19 km/11.8 mi*

MÍRES (146 C5) (*ⓜ J5*)

INSIDER TIP On Saturday mornings, a must for fans of weekly markets! This is where the region's farmers meet and take up (temporary) residence in the kafenía and fast-food restaurants, dine on souvláki and drink rakí. Street sellers have pomegranate juice and nuts for visitors, and the

In Míres everyone comes to the Saturday market

stalls sell all sorts of items ranging from imports from China to oil and fruits of the region, war toys to kitchen appliances – anything and everything that will make a little money. *13 km/8.1 mi*

PITSÍDIA (146 C5) (*ω H6*)

Are you more the backpack type of tourist? Then the cosy platía of this little inland village is just the place for you. The *Café Synántisi (daily from 8am | Budget)* has been a meeting place for relaxed guests (who often bring their own guitar or lyre with them) for generations. It's easy to hitchhike to Mátala and Kómo Beach, which is about 2.5 km/1.5 mi away. A pleasant, quiet place to stay is the *Pension Pátelo (12 rooms | tel. 28 92 04 50 00 | www. patelo-pitsidia.com | Budget)* at the upper end of the village. *4 km/2.5 mi*

VÓRI (146 C5) (*ω J5*)

Don't like chaos? Then you'll be happy at the Vóris *Museum of Ethnology (Apr–Oct daily from 11am-5pm | admission 3 euros)*. Traditional costumes and weapons, crafts, agricultural and kitchen equipment from the last 200 years are beautifully arranged here in cabinets labelled with Prussian accuracy. Afterwards, you'll realise just how much pleasanter life is today. *14 km/8.7 mi*

ZARÓS (147 D4) (*ω J5*)

This large town on the 340 m/1115 ft high southern slope of the Ída Mountain is well known for its trout farming and its many beautiful hiking possibilities. Two good trout tavernas (*Moderate*) are situated on the road to the little mountain lake of Záros. *25 km/15.5 mi*

ÁGIOS NIKÓLAOS

Shabby chic not your thing? Then Mirabéllo Bay should be the perfect holiday region for you. Even the Venetians once called it that: lovely sight. Everything here is beautifully looked after and spotlessly clean. And there's a good reason why Crete's tourism began here in the early 1970s. Walt Disney, Jules Dassin and Mélina Merkoúri were among the first guests in the lovely bay.

Countless other hotels have been added to the early luxury establishments on the outskirts of Ágios Nikólaos, at Ístro and Eloúnda, where celebrities from all over the world like to come on holiday and even play golf. Which is why Ágios Nikólaos as a town and the other, smaller resorts by the sea

are so beautifully presented. However, there's also plenty of affordable accommodation for the average, normal family here.

Completely normal Crete awaits you in the hilly hinterland. There, you will encounter flocks of sheep and goats on the road, see the older generation sitting in the old-fashioned cafenía, as they have always done. On the Lassíthi Plateau, a mule might carry you up to the cave where Zeus was born, or you can enjoy a boat trip to Spinalónga, which until recently was Europe's last leper colony. The little-visited excavation sites of Lató and Goúrnia tell you about Crete's history of long ago, while things become metaphysical at the monastery of Faneroménis.

Photo: Ágios Nikólaos harbour

Sleepy villages: the hinterland beyond the Mirabéllo Gulf region has retained its unspoilt rural Cretan character

ÁGIOS NIKÓLAOS

MAP INSIDE BACK COVER
(149 E3–4) *(ltl O4)* The little town that the locals simply call "Ágios" for short manages something of a balancing act: despite having more than 20,000 beds for visitors, even at peak season Ágios Nikólaos is never like an overrun tourist spot. As the administrative capital for eastern Crete, is extremely independent – and unlike Iráklio, Chaniá and Réthimno never lets you feel as if you were in a capital.

The cafés on the shore of the small inland lake are only one centre; the streams of tourists are also drawn to the many cafés along the long coastal road that surrounds an entire rocky peninsula, the harbour front as well as the inviting shops in the pedestrian zone. Ágios (pop. 27,000), has developed organically, if haphazardly and not always imaginatively.

The town is at its most beautiful on the shore of the small lake *Límni Vulisméni,* which since 1870 has been connected to the town's harbour by a channel. It is surrounded by tales and legends. Fifty years ago, after the last eruption

AGÍA TRIÁDA CHURCH

Are these angels vegetarians? Possibly. The tiny carrot in the modern mosaics above the portal to the main church

Agía Triáda church: this new mosaic is classically Byzantine

of the Santorini volcano, the lake water foamed and rose up, and dead fish washed ashore. Since then, some Cretans believe that there is an underground connection between the lake and the ocean.

Fishing boats are on the lake, which is surrounded by rocky cliffs on two sides. Here you will also find tables and chairs set out by taverna and café owners. Just as nice are the cafés up at the cliff top, where you have a view of the lake and the harbour. At night, the eastern side is the busiest.

could be a reference to the eating habits of the three little angels that Abraham and his wife Sarah are looking after. Or, on the other hand, to a preference of the mosaic artist.

The many large-scale wall murals inside the church tell other biblical stories, with more details for you to encode. If you know a little bit about it, you'll have a wonderful time here. Unlike most medieval wall murals, these new frescoes in the traditional Byzantine style are easy to identify. *Mostly 7am–noon and 4pm–7.30pm | admission free*

ARCHAEOLOGICAL MUSEUM

The people of Antiquity lived in uncertain times: they could never be sure that the world would still be all right a year later, or that the soil would bring forth food for them. That was why they honoured fertility goddesses. And they imagined them to be like the goddess of Mírtos, who can be seen in the Archaeological Museum. Her insignificant head sits on a long, phallic neck. Far more important that that are the two added breasts and (painted) triangle of her pubic area, while her spindly arms likewise fade into insignificance. Also interesting: a clay house model illustrated how people lived here around 3250 years ago. And that they believed in life after death is confirmed by a very special skull from the 1st century. It is displayed here as it was found: surrounded by a wreath of thin golden leaves and with a coin in the mouth. The deceased needed this to pay Charon, the ferryman on the river to the kingdom of the dead. *Tue–Sun 8am–3pm | admission 4 euros | Odós Paleológu 68*

FOOD & DRINK

AVLÍ

Being in this cosy taverna is almost like being in the countryside. You sit under a green canopy of leaves away from the noise and bustle, drink wine from a barrel and enjoy the rustic cuisine. If the host has time, he will be pleased to join you for a chat. *Daily noon–3pm and from 7pm | Odós Pring. Georgíou 12 | Moderate*

ÍTANOS

Although sitting here is nicer in the evenings, this unpretentious taverna is perfect for a quick, very good lunch with the locals. It is in a central location, close to the town's main square. The Cretan dishes are freshly prepared every day, and presented appetisingly in heated containers. You'll only need the menu to find out the prices. The offer depends heavily on the season, and it's excellent value for money. *Daily from 11am-11pm | Odós Kípru 1 | Budget*

MIGÓMIS ⚠

Romantics will love this taverna high above the sea: every evening, a skilled pianist is here to provide the musical entertainment. Half the tables on the open veranda are elegantly laid, the other half is for guests who only want a drink. The menu is international, and includes duck breast and salmon. *Daily from 11am | Odós Nikolaou Plastíra 20 | www.migomis.gr | Expensive*

PÉLAGOS

The traditional fishing boat on the terrace of this classic villa indicates what is best here: fresh fish. Which is on ice onboard this *kaikis*. You can enjoy it in what is probably the prettiest taverna garden in the town.

★ **Goúrnia**
See how the Minoans lived: the ruins of a 3500-year old city, open to all citizens
→ p. 79

★ **Lassíthi Plateau**
A fertile mountain oasis with ancient caves, beautiful villages and a folk museum
→ p. 80

★ **Spinalónga**
A lepers' village built within the walls of a Venetian fortress → p. 83

MARCO POLO HIGHLIGHTS

The furnishings are coloured, while the grilled squid with honey and fennel is a tender poem. *Daily noon–midnight | Odós Stratigú Koráka 10 | Expensive*

SHOPPING

BLANC DU NIL
You'll leave this boutique all in white (but not carrying a bouquet). Everything in it is white – cool white blouses, shirts, dresses, trousers. The only material is the finest quality Egyptian cotton. No wedding dresses, though. *Odós Sfakianáki 9*

DES
Hand-made fashion jewellery is the speciality of Déspina Korneláki. Coloured stones and feathers are her favourite elements. *Odós 5is Merarchías 13*

KERÁ
Lovely shop with tastefully selected items (both new and old); woven articles, jewellery, marionettes and dolls from Greek workshops. *Odós J. Kundurú 8 | at the harbour underneath the restaurant Cretan Stars*

MARKET
A large weekly market takes place every Wednesday morning on *Odós Ethnikís Antistáseo street* which starts on the lakeshore.

BEACHES

The most beautiful beach in town is the almost 120 m/394 ft long pebble *Kitroplatía beach*, about 5 minutes from the harbour. Along the coastal road to Eloúnda, at the edge of town, lies the sandy *Havanía beach*. Almost 1.5 km/0.9 mi south-east of the town, you will find the 250 m/820 ft long sandy *Almirós beach*, about a mile further along the road to

Sitía lies the sandy 100 m/328 ft long *Ammoudará beach*. An easy and cheap way of visiting the beaches of Kaló Chorió and Ístro further to the east is with the public bus service. Tavernas, deckchairs and umbrellas can be found on all of these beaches.

ENTERTAINMENT

Mega discos are out; they no longer exist. In Ágios, people prefer to spend the nights in the many smaller bars along the road around the peninsula, between the harbour and Kitroplatía Beach. Plenty of dancing there especially when parties are announced on the notice board and on Facebook.

ALÉXANDROS
Music bar in a roof garden with a view of the lake, lushly decorated with flowers. Dance music for every age and taste which sometimes makes older guests look back on the stories of their lives nostalgically, as the DJ will play oldies on request. Drinks on offer include Spanish sangria and Greek champagne. *Daily from 8pm | Odós Kondiláki 1*

YIANNI'S ROCK BAR ⅍
Owner and DJ Yianni still plays CDs for music. Let's rock! is his motto, and he's always happy to oblige with requests. Look beyond your immediate surroundings, and you'll see the sea. *Odós I. Kundúru 1*

INSIDER TIP PERÍPOU
This culture café high above the lake also sells CDs and books as well as being a cultural stage. Locals and tourists mingle from 10pm with wine and cocktails. The music selection ranges from Greek songwriters to hard techno. *Daily from 10pm | Odós 28is Octovríou 25*

ÁGIOS NIKÓLAOS

WHERE TO STAY

DU LAC

Do you also like to spend a few hours in your room during the day or evening? Then book a room with a ☆ balcony and sea views in the only hotel on Lake Vulisméni. Your home from home will be 215 ft² in the middle of the town, with lots of lovely things to look at, and you can enjoy your bottle of wine at a better price than in the expensive places «down there». *24 rooms | Odós 28is Octovríou 17 | tel. 28 41 02 27 11 | www. dulachotel.gr | Budget*

INSIDER TIP PALAZZO

If you appreciate modern technology but also appreciate an old-fashioned interior, then stay in one of the ten 2-room apartments on Kitroplatía Beach. ☆ Eight apartments with sea views, all with a kitchenette with coffee maker, fridge and microwave. *Odós Tselépi 18/Aktí Pagkálou | tel. 28 41 02 50 80 | www.palazzo-apartments.gr | Moderate*

SGOÚROS

The only hotel on the town's Kitroplatía Beach may be a getting on a bit, but it's in the best shape – and it's only 50 steps from the hotel door to the water. *28 rooms. | Odós N. Pagalú 3 | tel. 28 41 02 89 31 | www.sgourosgrouphotels. com | Budget–Moderate*

INFORMATION

MUNICIPAL TOURIST INFORMATION OFFICE
On the bridge between the lake and the harbour | tel. 28 41 02 23 57 | www.aghio snikolaos.eu

Is it evening yet? The taverns blend charmingly against Lake Límni Vulisméni

77

WHERE TO GO

ELOÚNDA (149 E3) (*𝄐 O4*)

Blue-bloods and celebrities from all over the world often only know one place on Crete: unassuming Eloúnda. Leonardo di Caprio and Lady Gaga are only two of the big names that have already holidayed here. Nowhere else on Crete will you find so many luxurious hotels of the highest (price) ratings so close together. Private pools and butler service are as much of a matter of course as helicopter transfers and luxury yachts for day trips. But you wouldn't think it from looking at the place. The luxury hotels are unobtrusive, away from the village, and the better-known hotel guests prefer to stay anonymous in their cages. If you'd still like to see them, are not staying in the same hotel but are willing to spend a lot of money, then book a table in one of the hotel restaurants such as Peruvian-Japanese *Mistura (tel. 28 41 06 70 00 | www. eloundabeach.gr | Expensive* at the hotel *Eloúnda Beach* or treat yourself to a session in one of the luxury spas. The loveliest one is at the *Blue Palace Resort (tel. 28 41 06 55 00 | www.bluepalace.gr | Expensive)*. Ordinary citizens appreciate the 400-m/1300-ft long promenade, flanked by tavernas, from the tiny harbour to the dam on the large island *Spinalónga* (not the same as the leper colony), which passes through former saltworks. In the flat waters, snorkelers can still explore the remains of the ancient town of *Oloús*, of which there still remains an early Christian floor mosaic right behind the *Canal Bar. 12 km/7.5 mi*

FANEROMÉNIS MONASTERY (151 D2) (*𝄐 Q4*)

Even the drive here is an experience: the cul-de-sac up to the monastery includes lots of hairpin bends and potholes. Goats and sheep are in no hurry to move out of the way, and sometimes will even take food from your hand. Only 9 km/5.6 mi to your destination: at a height of 400 m/1300 ft, the monastery, which was built over 300 years ago, nestles against

CRETAN MULTITASKER

On the road from Ágios Nikólaos to the Lassíthi Plateau, Manólis Farsáris has established a tourist supermarket in the nearly uninhabited village of Zénia. Every year he builds another room by himself. There is even a bar and café where he serves *rakómeli* (*rakí* mixed with honey) as well as ice cream, snacks and fresh juice. In the shop section he sells anything from Korean jeans to cheap icons and spoons carved by himself during the winter. But he also offers his guests another little service: on the pavement outside he has set up a pair of binoculars on an old umbrella stand with a picture that he drew himself in which he details everything that you can see through the binoculars. Next to it he has some slingshots hanging from a branch of a tree for children to play with. A few feet away a multilingual handwritten sign tells you that the tables and chairs on the terrace can be used at no cost for picnics if you bring your own picnic baskets. Manólis has to feed his family and he is attempting to do so in his own unique Cretan way!

The monks in the Faneroménis monastery are not always home since they also visit local inhabitants

a rock face. Today, only a few monks still live here, with their dogs and cats. They are pleased to show the (few) visitors they have the church built into a large grotto, and usually serve them coffee, rakí and biscuits for refreshment. *Mon–Sat 8am–1pm, daily 4pm–7pm. 23 km/14.3 mi*

GOÚRNIA ★ ☆ (149 F4) (∅ O–P5)
On the coastal road on a low hill above the Gulf of Mirabéllo are the excavations of the Minoan city of Goúrnia. The foundation walls of the 3500 year old houses are in good condition and parts of the stairways that led to the upper floor can still be seen. Narrow, paved alleys lead to the former palace on the top of the hill. *Tue–Sun 8.30am–3pm | admission 4 euros | 19 km/11.8 mi*

KASTÉLLI (149 E3) (∅ O4)
With its old Venetian mansions and artfully wrought gates and railings, this very quiet village is one of the most beautiful in the region. Its narrow streets are full of wild geraniums.

An alley lined with eucalyptus trees leads you into the neighbouring village of *Fourní,* where almond trees blossom at the end of March. Here at the village square María Sfiráki awaits you in her tavern *Plátanos (daily from 8am | Budget)* underneath an old plane tree where she serves fresh salads and affordable dishes like rabbit or lamb's liver.

A track leads to the excavations of the Dorian city of *Dríros,* where the remains of an Apollo temple, cistern, altar and the Agorá can still be seen. *Admission free | 20 km/12.4 mi*

KATHARÓ PLATEAU
(149 D4) (∅ N5)
Do you want to escape completely from the noise and bustle? then this high plain, completely isolated at an altitude of 1150 m/3770 ft, is the perfect destination for you. There is a road of about 17 km/10.6 mi, almost completely asphalted, up from *Krítsa.* The plateau

(owned by Krítsa municipality) is used to farm fruit, grapes and grains. People only live here between 20 May and 30 November, and during this time the *kafenía* and tavernas are also open. An important festival of the Virgin Mary is celebrated on the 6th of August. *28 km/17.4 mi*

KRÍTSA (149 E4) (*ω O5*)

This lovely mountain village is sometimes completely overrun by visitors, and has plenty of souvenir shops, cafés and tavernas as well as a Byzantine art jewel at the bottom edge of the village right on the road from Ágios: the *Panagía i Kerá* church *(only April–Oct Tue–Sun 8.30am–3pm | admission 3 euros)* with perfectly intact frescoes dating from the 15th to 17th century. The dome in the nave does not show Christ as the ruler of all, instead there are four scenes from the New Tes-

tament: Mary in the temple, the baptism of Jesus, the resurrection of Lazarus and Jesus' entrance into Jerusalem on Palm Sunday. In the centre of the dome, four angels represent heaven. The prophets of the Old Testament that prophesised the coming of Christ are depicted on the lower edge. The pendentives connecting the dome to the nave show, as is often the case, the apostles Matthew, Mark, Luke and John. Their gospels spread the teachings of Jesus to the people. Even for those not interested in theology, the images of hell on the west wall will leave a strong impression. *9 km/5.6 mi*

LASSÍTHI PLATEAU ★
(148–149 C–E 3–4) (*ω M–N 4–5*)

A day without the sea can also be pleasant. Perhaps even so pleasant, that you make the spontaneous decision to spend

The sea at your back: it can be easy to forget about swimming on the rural Lassíthi plateau

a night in the pure rural idyll on Crete's biggest high plain. It's certainly possible. From *Stalída* (148 C2) *(M4)* on the coastal motorway, an excellent road winds up in generous bends to the foothills of the Díkti Mountains. A look back at the coast will amaze you: how delightfully small are even the big Cretan tourist centres Chersónisos and Mália, compared with those on Spanish or Turkish coasts! The first mountain village, *Mochós*, welcomes you with one of the prettiest village squares on Crete – and it's time for your first coffee. In *Krasí* you'll see the island's oldest plane tree on the square with the large Venetian fountain. At the *Kerá Kardiótissa Monastery (daily from 8am–6pm | admission 2 euros)* you'll admire the icon of the Blessed Virgin Mary – a keen traveller: according to the legend, she was taken to Istan-

bul by Turks no fewer than three times, but every time she made it back home by herself. On her last flight, she allegedly not only brought the chain, but the pillar that the Turks had chained her to as well. They can also be seen in the monastery: the chain on the icon in the church, and the pillar in the cloisters. Then comes the *Museum of Mankind (daily from 9am-6pm | admission 4 euros)*. A former customs officer tells you, in a charmingly naïve way, how he imagines the development of mankind from the earliest Stone Age to the moon landing.

At lunchtime, you'll be at the top of the *Àmbelos Afín* (148 C3) *(M4)* pass, where the eponymous restaurant *(daily from 11.30am | Moderate)* already has a delicious pork roast waiting for you. It is served with potatoes from the Lassíthi high plain. This plateau, which is surrounded by high mountains, is 10 km/6.2 mi long and 5 km/3.1 mi wide. More than 20 villages are arranged around the perimeter to waste as little as possible of the fertile soil.

The drive from the top of the pass to the 800-m/2600-ft plain takes only three minutes, and you'll be greeted by a few fabric-covered wind turbines. You can see them in old photos in all the tavernas up here: until well into the 1970s, there were thousands of these wind turbines on the Lassíthi, where they were used to draw up the groundwater. Now they have almost all been replaced by motor-driven pumps. The main destination for the many tourist buses up here is the *Diktéon Ándron stalactite cave (daily 9am–3pm, May–Sept sometimes until 7pm | admission 4 euros)* above the village of *Psychró* (148 C4) *(N5)*. This was a place of worship from as early as the 2nd century BC. According to legend, it was here that Zeus was brought up by goats because his mother Rhea feared that his father Kronos would see him as a rival and devour him as he had Zeus' siblings. It is possible to ride up to the cave on mules. The cave is well lit and sturdy footwear is recommended.

However, as an individual traveller, Lassíthi has so much more to offer you. You can stroll through the peaceful, largely unspoilt villages, enjoy short walks around the fields, and just experience the pure rusticity. In the large village *Ágios Geórgios* there is also an interesting folk museum with an adjacent gallery *(daily 10am–4pm | admission 3 euros)*. The holiday homes INSIDERTIP *Vilaéti* in the neighbouring village of Ágios Konstantínos *(5 houses | tel. 28 44 03 19 83 | www.vilaeti.gr | Expensive)* have a museum-like feel. A local family has lovingly restored the old village houses and decorated them with traditional details. Those who stay here sleep in an environment that harks back to a bygone era and can also enjoy various Lassíthian specialities at the ⚫ *Taverna Villaéti (daily from noon*

| *Moderate)* which belongs to the same family and is situated on the main road. The sister of the proprietor is one of the pioneers of the organic potato cultivation on the plateau. *45 km/28 mi*

LATÓ ⚓ (149 E4) (*ɯ O4*)

Once upon a time, princes had ruins built in their parks because it looked so romantic. However, on the green hill of Lató, history really was the architect. A small theatre, the foundations of an old temple, the tiny, antique market square, a cistern, the ruins of old houses and the town wall are all that is left of the town that thrived here between the 7th and 4th centuries BC. Today they are the perfect spot for a picnic. *April–Oct, Tue–Sun 8.30am–3pm | admission 3 euros. 3 km/1.9 mi*

PRÍNA (149 E5) (*ɯ O5*)

Would you like a private concert? Then make sure your MARCO POLO is clearly visible on your table at the taverna INSIDERTIP *Pitópoulis (daily from 11am | Budget)*, because host Dímitris is a well-known lýra player. Once a week (usually on Wednesday), he spends a whole evening playing for locals and other guests – and he'll be pleased to play you a few notes from his repertoire, provided his wife Stélla is happy on her own in the kitchen. *19 km/11.8 mi*

SÍSI (149 D2) (*ɯ N3*)

A little Figuera on Mallorca, a touch of Norway and a generous dash of Crete – Sísi is an exceptional place. The centre is a mini fjord, where you can swim among the fishing boats. Palms reach up into the sky on the western shore, while on the other side people enjoy a glass or cup of something on the terraces of the cafés and bars. At the western exit to the fjord is a small sandy beach, and to the east there are a few fish tavernas on the quay.

No mercy: people afflicted by leprosy were simply left to fend for themselves in Spinalónga's medieval fortress

Hosts Níkos and Michális at *Angístri (daily from 11am | Moderate) are delightful*. If you're not too bothered about the fjord, walk 1–2 km/0.6–1.2 mi east, where there are more sandy/shingle beaches. The hotel *Porto Sísi (15 apartments | tel. 28 41 07 13 85 | www.portosisi.com | Moderate)* is situated close to the village centre and directly on the coast and is a good accommodation option. If you prefer hotels that also offer sporting activities, then the resort hotel *Kaliméra Kríti (455 rooms | tel. 28 41 06 90 00 | www.kalimerakriti.gr | Expensive)* 1 km/0.6 mi to the east is a good option. *22 km/13.7 mi*

SPINALÓNGA ★ ☼
(149 F2–3) (*ᗰ O3–4*)

The Venetian fortress island Spinalónga *(Kalidón)* made its tourist career as the "Island of Lepers": between 1913 and 1957, it was a leper colony. The afflicted lived amongst the medieval walls in total isolation in a village they built themselves, and were also buried here. Amongst the lepers were craftsmen and farmers, a hairdresser and even a priest; people married and had children. But healthy newborn babies were immediately taken from their mothers and sent to an orphanage in Crete. Apart from the sporadic visits of a doctor the lepers had no medical care at all. The road around the island is only about 1 km/0.6 mi long.

The trip out by excursion boat is worthwhile not only to experience a slight shiver while visiting the island, but also because of the diverse coastal scenery. INSIDER TIP Taking part in a tour with an English guide is recommended, the guides bring the past to life with their retelling of the island's gruesome history. *Daily boats from Ágios (12–17 euros), Eloúnda (10 euros) and Pláka (8 euros) | admission 8 euros, guided tour 2 euros*

IERÁPETRA

On the radio, Arabic music mixes with Cretan sounds while winds from the south blow in dust from the Sahara. In the centre of old town Ierápetra a minaret towers upwards, there are hints of northern Africa everywhere in the landscape.

Ierápetra and its region is an unusual part of Crete, an area that is completely different from the other regions on the island.

While Ierápetra very often suffers from the heat in the summer, it is an ideal holiday destination during the winter so life bustles here throughout the whole year. You can swim in the Libyan Sea even during December and January.

The coastal region of Ierápetra extends up to the Messará Plain, which borders on the 1231 m/4040 ft high Asterússia Mountains in the south. The only area well developed for tourism is between Mírtos and Makrigialós; the remaining coastal resorts are far below the main roads, and exclusively destinations for individual tourists who are not bothered by beaches that are more shingle than sand, and myriads of greenhouses, either intact or destroyed by the wind. Good beaches, mostly with coarse sand, are found mainly on the coastal strips between Ierápetra and Makrigialós. True bathing havens are the islands of Chrisí and Koufonísi off the south coast, which are the destinations for excursion boats in summer. Both are uninhabited, and have the finest sandy beaches and no hotels at all. In fact, there isn't even a

A touch of Africa: greenhouses, mountain villages and lonely beaches – you can winter very well in the warmth of southern Crete

taverna on Koufonísi – although it does have a town with a theatre that is slowly sinking into the sand.

IERÁPETRA

(149 F6) (*ळ O6*) **In the beauty scale of Cretan towns, Ierápetra (pop. 27,600) is happy to be last. There are other interests here. All that count are the early vegetables. The beach and tourism are peripherals.**

Back in 1965, Paul Cooper from Holland showed the farmers here how to grow cucumbers and tomatoes in greenhouses. They became the richest farmers in the whole of Greece. For a time, there was also talk of building a private airport to get the early vegetables to European markets more quickly. Even today, the plastic-covered *thermokípia* reach as far as the outskirts of the town, sparkling like a huge lake in the sunlight.

Almost every vehicle in the little town is a pick-up, because being the shopping

A touch of the old town: the restored well house and an old minaret on a quiet platía

centre for the farmers is Ierápetra's main function.

SIGHTSEEING

OLD TOW

Idyll in Ierápetra? You guessed it: nope! But at least there is a very quiet quarter, where the town's Turks lived until 1913. You can easily spend an hour strolling around there. Start at the western end of the beach promenade. There is a tiny ☆ fortress *(Tue-Sun 8am-3pm | admission free)* that was built by the Venetians in 1626 with views of the old town and harbour from the battlements. Then set course for the minaret you just spotted. It belongs to a permanently locked *mosque* with a well house on its square that has already been restored.

Then stroll back to the beach promenade, where a discreet signpost next to the *Levante* taverna indicates the *Napoleon House*. You can't go inside, but do look at it from the outside. It is said that Napoleon spent a night here in 1798 on his foray into Egypt.

ARCHAEOLOGICAL MUSEUM

If you've succumbed to the Minos virus or make pottery yourself, then you'll enjoy visiting this little museum in what was once a Turkish school. It has two Minoan potter's wheels and a lovely Minoan sarcophagus with hunting scenes. The section with three Minoans in a cart that is being pulled by animals is unique. The cart is on spoked rather than disc wheels – and we're talking more than 3300 years ago! *Tue–Sun 8am–3pm | admission*

2 euros | Odós Ethnikís Antistáseos | close to the square in the new town

FOOD & DRINK

I SKÉDIA

White taverna by the sea on the outskirts of the town in the direction of Sitía. Floating cloths and ships' ropes for decoration, bamboo for the roof. George and Helen keep their taverna open all year round, and many of the locals are regulars who appreciate the authentic Cretan cuisine and excellent value for money. *Daily from 1pm | east of the hotel Petra Mare | Budget–Moderate*

INSIDER TIP LEVANTE

When the lovely smell of freshly grilled fish streams out of the kitchen, it practically pulls the sun-worshippers on the beach outside this restaurant off their towels. Vegetarians will also find plenty to enjoy in the friendly, rather chic taverna. Host Níkos thinks his moussaká is the best. *Daily from 11am | Odós Stratigoú Samouíl 38 | www.ierapetra.net/levante | Budget*

INSIDER TIP PÓRTEGO

Bar, café and restaurant in 100-year old buildings with small and atmospheric inner courtyards. Good variety of typical *mesédes*. *Daily from 7.30pm | Odós N. Foniadáki 8 | Expensive*

SHOPPING

MARKET (LAIKÍ AGORÁ)

How farmers shop: the Saturday market in the east of the town is not aimed at tourists. *Odós Psilináki*

SPORTS

A water sports school on Ierápetra's beach offers you courses in windsurfing, water-skiing and sailing; canoes and paddle boats can also be hired. You can also book diving courses here.

ENTERTAINMENT

The cafés and bars along the beach promenade are at their liveliest before midnight. After midnight, revellers withdraw to the *Privilege (from 10pm)*, where the DJ mostly plays Greek rock. Locals also like to drive into the villages in the evenings: Music bars and nightclubs can be found mainly in the *Odós Kirvá* behind the beachfront promenade *(e.g. Seven, Saxo, Insomnia)*. 5 km/3.1 mi inland in the village of *Vaínia* at the *Ouzeri Plátanos (closed Mon)* on the village square you can enjoy a simple table wine and Cretan *mesédes* under mulberry trees.

WHERE TO STAY

INSIDER TIP CRETAN VILLA

It's not possible to have more local colour: This small two-storey guest house with a tiny inner courtyard was built during the 19th century and was once the town's first hospital. Its proprietor, a true local patriot, has decorated it in Cretan style and takes good care of his guests. *9 rooms | Odós Oplárchu Lakérda 16 | tel. 28 42 02 85 22 | www.cretan-villa.com | Budget–Moderate*

PETRA MARE

C'est la vie: to the rest of the world, this is an absolute eyesore – a hotel block that can be seen for miles and miles. And yet its residents find it extremely pleasant. A pedestrian promenade leads into the town centre about 800 m/2600 ft further, while to the east is a long pebble beach. If at all possible, book a room with a sea view! *223 rooms | coastal road east of the centre | tel. 28 42 02 33 41 | www.petramare.com | Moderate*

WHERE TO GO

CHRISÍ ISLAND ★ (150 A6) (*Ø O7*)

It's not possible to have more sand. The island of Chrisí was virtually made for days in the sun. Besides a taverna, a beach bar and dunes above which the bizarre roots and branches of the 10 m/32.8 ft high prickly juniper trees tower, there are also long white sandy beaches. Excursion and taxi boats come here daily from Ierápetra during the summer. Staying overnight is prohibited, but many young Greeks do not adhere to this rule – probably because there is no police station. Nude bathing is as common as partying on the beach at night, although almost nobody takes the 3-hour trekking route around the island which offers no shade along the way.

KAPSÁ MONASTERY ★ ☼ (151 D4) (*Ø Q5*)

It's unusual to find monasteries right beside the sea. This one is in a particularly lovely spot: it was built in the 15th century, partly into a rock face. There are few visitors, and the peace is heavenly. Including on the tiny shingle beach with old tamarisks just below the monastery. *Daily from 8am-noon and 4pm–7pm. 46 km/28.6 mi*

INSIDER TIP KOUFONÍSI (151 E5) (*Ø R6*)

The ancient Romans bred purple snails on the island to produce a dye that they used to colour the emperor's robes. In those days, Koufonísi even had a small, ultra-rich town with its own theatre. Now, like every other ancient building, it is slowly sinking into the sand, which is the perfect finishing touch to the island's charms. Apart from that, the only thing to do here is swim: on any of its 36 white beaches with extremely fine

SEE YOU TOMORROW

Buses, ships and planes keep to the official schedules but in everyday Cretan life, punctuality is not a necessity. Cretans seldom arrange to meet at an exact time, but prefer to be vague with *áwrio* = tomorrow, *to proí* = morning, *to apógewma* = afternoon (from about 4pm) or *to wrádi* = at night (from about 8pm). If you as a guest accept this trait you will save yourself a lot of trouble.

Move a short distance away from the mooring, and you won't even have to share Koufonísi's beaches with fishermen

sand, and where the water shimmers in flat bays in every imaginable shade of blue and turquoise. Just 15 minutes from the mooring point, you'll be able to spend a few hours pretending you are Robinson Crusoe. In summer, the boat trips by *Cretan Daily Cruises (www.cretandaily cruises.com)* to Koufonísi almost all leave from Makrigialós, travelling time about 60 minutes.

LÉNDAS ★ ⚓ (147 D6) *(𝄞 J6)*

Just keep away from the mass tourism has always been the watchword for backpacking tourists. Yet they've been coming here themselves in droves for 50 years now, without ever noticing that they, too, have become a mass. Whatever: this very isolated little place on the south coast takes excellent care of its clientele, leaving many things as they are. Today, though, guests no longer stay in the grandparents' emptied-out bedrooms or huts, but in modern guestrooms and studios, still hold hands in the cosy beach tavernas, swim naked on Dískos Beach and drink wine on terraces right over the water. History has even left a little bit of culture: on the outskirts of the village are the ruins of a *Roman shrine to Asclepius* (Tue-Sun 9am-3pm | admission free), the god of medicine. This coastal village, which is popular amongst young independent travellers and campers only has a few houses and tavernas. The whitewashed houses are surrounded by beautiful flower gardens and there is a short sand and pebble beach in front of the village. A 15 minute walk brings you to a sandy beach where nude bathing is common. *90 km/55.9 mi*

MAKRÍGIALOS (150 C4) (*ळ Q5*)

The village street is superfluous if you holiday here. Just follow the miles-long beach, and eventually you'll end up at almost every taverna in the village and, above all, at the harbour, where the excursion boat leaves for Koufonísi. The beach is fringed by tamarisks that provide shade, and you'll be perfectly comfortable among the boats in the taverna *To Stéki tou Miná (Mina's Place) (daily from 9am | Budget)*, which is also frequented by the fishermen. The only reason you'll have to go inland is to humour your inner history researcher. In the centre of Makrígialos, close to the village church, lie the foundations of an ancient Roman villa from the 1st century (with free access). Just outside the village in the direction of Ierápetra a brown roadsign shows the way to the remains of a late Minoan villa. A highly original place to stay close to nature is the INSIDER TIP *White River Cottages (13 houses | tel. 28 43 05 11 20 | www.whiterivercottages.com | Moderate)* in a narrow, very green valley about 1 km/0.6 mi from the coast. Refurbished labourer's cottages with stone floors and wooden ceilings are available to rent. They are decorated in true Cretan style. There is a small pool in the middle of vegetation. The path to the village and the beach is very dark at night, so a torch is a necessity. *24 km/14.9 mi*

MÍRTOS ☙ (149 D6) (*ळ N6*)

It is said that the wind hardly ever blows in Mírtos. And the coarse sand on the long beach doesn't stick to the skin. It's impossible to get lost in this hamlet; you can't miss a thing on the short beach promenade. If you holiday here, it's because you want to swim, swim and swim some more – and not have to choose from too many cafés, bars and tavernas in the evenings. Still, should you fall victim to a yearning for activity, there are two archaeological sites close by that are within walking distance.

Close to the village, on the hills of *Foúrnu Kórfi* and *Pírgos*, archaeologists have uncovered the remains of an early Minoan villa with about 90 rooms and a double storey building. Both sites are open to visitors and can be reached by following the brown signs on the coastal road from Ierápetra. It is only possible to get there on foot and both ascents start directly at their respective signpost. *15 km/9.3 mi*

PÉFKI (150 C4) (*ळ Q5*)

You go to Péfki if you're staying close by or happen to be driving through. Why? For a pleasant visit to the excellent, cosy cafenío *Zur Weinstube (daily from 9am | Budget)* in the village centre. At the front

LOW BUDGET

Everybody along the promenade on the island of Chrisí wants to make money from the excursion boats. Tickets for the trip are sold on the boat, at travel agencies and tavernas. The competition is fierce but that means that families or small groups can negotiate prices under 25 euros.

Outside of the peak season, the coastal villages west of Ierápetra offer rooms from 26 euros, like Venetía *(tel. 28 91 09 22 58)* in Tsoútsouros.

you sit under vine tendrils, at the back with views of a gorge that goes into the sea. The hosts put rakí, wine, cheese and olive on the table, cook a hearty omelette, and in summer also serve a small selection of dishes of the day. Two hours spent here are pure perfection. *28 km/17.4 mi*

INSIDER TIP ▶ BUTTERFLY GORGE
(150 B5) (*Ø P6*)

Feel like a spot of climbing and stream crossing? Your enjoyable endeavours will be rewarded by large numbers of butter-

1 km/0.6 mi to the west of the village of Koutsoúra *(Communal Park of Koutsoura* or *Dasaki Butterfly Gorge* on the signs)*. You can walk the gorge between May and November. *20 km/12.4 mi*

BRAMIANÁ RESERVOIR
(149 E5) (*Ø O5*)

Built in 1986, this reservoir at Gra Ligiá has a capacity of 16 million litres of water and is the second largest in Crete. It irrigates the many greenhouses in the region. During the winter it is a bird paradise with more than 200 species of birds.

Four standing, one sitting – in Mírtos

flies and a few small waterfalls. You'll need good shoes, and a towel is useful in case you miss your footing. There's no destination; you just turn back when you feel like it. Good idea: take a picnic with you. The walk starts at the car park

They include spotted eagles, snake eagles, peregrine falcons, bitterns, herons, pink flamingos and ibis. You can hike around the whole reservoir and there are observation points for amateur ornithologists. *5 km/3.1 mi*

SITÍA

East and west are more than just directions on Crete. They're world views. Both extremes of the island have their very loyal fans. By far the majority prefers the west. The outermost east is extreme in a different way: no high mountains, but with plenty of appealing, African-style landscapes, rich red soil, small canyons, stony plains and a few palm trees. The towns are insignificant and relatively new. What count are the quaint villages and often unusual beaches.

Even the mentality of the people here seems to be a little different: there are almost no bullet holes in the road signs, indicating that the Cretan resistance to foreign rule is no longer an issue here. But the sound of the *lýra* can still be heard, especially at festivals, where the instrument lies ready for use in many a taverna.

The region is still undiscovered by mass tourism. Only Sitía, which is the lively rural centre of the region, has a single hotel that is slightly larger. There are only a few beaches around here but they are very long and – apart from Vái beach with its palms – always still have lots of space.

There are only a few important historical sites and the Minoan palace of Káto Zákros sees more turtles than visitors. Thus, those taking a round trip of the island will also be able to relax here and enjoy the best this region has to offer: the stunning natural beauty and landscape.

Palm trees, lemons, raisins: in spring the air smells of herbs, in autumn the grapes are pressed – Crete's east is still pristine

SITÍA

(151 D2) *(𝕄 Q4)* **Sitía (pop. 18,300) could have been made for slowing down. It's unlikely that anyone here has ever experienced stress. A taverna's tables and chairs stand on the green strip of a four-lane highway – but the waiter is still the very picture of health.**

The town of Sitía starts directly at the east end of the beach promenade, where the cafés and restaurants draw all life to them.

The shops that are important to the locals are all within a distance of a few metres of the beach platía; the alleys that lead up to the castle are all residential areas full of flowers and cats. Even the harbour of Sitía is quiet. If there's someone who offers boat trips? For whom? A ferry twice a week, the occasional small freighter, that's it. Thank Zeus for e-books – and places to visit you can get to by service bus.

Living room under the lemon tree: the guesthouse Archontikó Is warm and friendly

SIGHTSEEING

ARCHAEOLOGICAL MUSEUM

Here's a young lad you should see! A Minoan carved him 3500 years ago out of ivory from a hippopotamus. He chiselled his fine hair out of serpentinite stone, and originally his eyes were mountain crystals. His physical beauty was matched by golden magnificence: sandals, bangles, belt and loincloth were made of gold leaf. You hardly notice that the pretty fellow is only 0.5 m/1.6 ft tall. *Tue–Sun 8am–3pm | admission 3 euros | at the town exit on the road towards Ierápetra*

FOOD & DRINK

THE BALCONY 🔊

Tónya Karandinoú likes to do things differently. Her restaurant is not by the sea, nor on the ground floor. It is, in fact, on the piano nobile, the bel étage, of a 19th century building. Tónya loves beautifully laid tables, Latin American music and crazy headwear, the French and Cretan cuisine. Which she refines creatively, using almost exclusively regional, ecologically grown, natural products. If you want to check carefully first to see if it's worth the investment, start with an aperitif with amuses gueules at the bar. And if you'd like a table, you're welcome to make a reservation. *Daily noon–3pm and 7pm–11pm | Odós Funtalídu 19 | www.balconyrestaurant.com | Expensive*

CRETAN HOUSE

Do you prefer to sit somewhere a little less exclusive, and instead be right by the water? Good run-of-the-mill Greek cuisine awaits you here – in large portions. The menu is extensive, and includes an excellent rabbit stifádo and a scampi gratin. There's often live Greek music on Saturdays. *Daily from 10am | Odós Karamanlí 1 | Moderate*

SHOPPING

MATTHAÍOS JEWELS

Matthaíos Karnakákis is from Sitía. He makes his silver, gold and platinum jewellery himself, but is inspired by Minoan and Byzantine originals. However, he has also found is own unique, often very playful modern line. As there are no in-betweens, the prices are extremely reasonable. *Odós Fountalídou 1 | www. matthaios-gold.com*

SITIAKÁ GLIKÁ ARÉTOUSA

Do you know what an ethnic grocery store is? To Anna Garefaláki, it's her little shop that specialises in products from the region. It includes lots of sweet things, and also has rakí, wine and oúzo on the shelves. *Odós El. Venizélou/Odós Daskalogiánni*

SPORTS & BEACHES

The town of Sitía itself is not recommended as a holiday destination for sports enthusiasts. The next water sport centre is as far away as Vái, about 25 km/15.5 mi. You can swim on the sandy beach (which has no shade) east of the town's edge, but it lies just beneath the very busy main road in the direction of Vái.

ENTERTAINMENT

Ultra-cool parties often develop quite spontaneously in the little bars along the harbour. However, there's no room for big discos.

BLACK HOLE

Thanks to its excellent cocktails, the Black Hole (seating inside and out) is always the no. 1 venue in town. Occasionally there is also live music. *Odós Karaveláki 7*

NOUVELLE BOUTIQUE

The audience is usually younger here than elsewhere, the music louder. Thanks to the in-house DJ. *Odós El. Venizélou 161*

WHERE TO STAY

INSIDER TIP ARCHONTIKÓ

Alexandra is an unusual woman. She is originally from Frankfurt, but hasn't left Sitía for years. She runs a guesthouse in the old town in a building that is over 100 years old. Alexandra doesn't like anonymity: she will only give a room to people who turn up at the door or make a booking by phone. This is to ensure that the guests and her establishment suit each other.

⭐ **Káto Zákros**
Not so far from the Middle East: Between a beach and a rocky wilderness lies a Minoan palace worth seeing → p. 98

⭐ **Vái**
Crete's famous palm grove beach. Very photogenic, but always crowded during peak season → p. 101

⭐ **Xerókambos**
Quite literally exclusive: hardly anyone has discovered the lovely beaches yet → p. 101

MARCO POLO HIGHLIGHTS

The small terrace under the lemon tree is a living room that is shared by everyone. Solo travellers can generally find a pleasant partner for walks and activities here. Guests prepare their own breakfasts, while the landlady serves coffee or herbal tea. *11 rooms, 10 of them with shared bathrooms | Odos I. Kondiláki 16 | tel. 28 43 02 81 72 | Budget*

ELYSEE

Do you want your own bathroom or are only staying for one night? Then this basic, modern hotel right beside the traffic-free esplanade is just the place for you. It also has a private car park. *26 rooms | Odós K. Karamanlí 14 | tel.*

LOW BUDGET

You can eat very inexpensively at Stéki *(daily from 11am | Odós Papandréou 7)*, a friendly taverna in Sitía where a half a litre of wine only costs 3.50 euros and spaghetti with grilled chicken only 4.50 euros (no cover charge!). Inside you can have a comfortable seat close to the television or outside with the locals on the green strip of the four-lane road.

You can team up with others and travel inexpensively on Crete. When taking a taxi from the airport to the city (or any other destination) get together with some other tourists and pretend to know each other. A taxi driver will charge just once if passengers know one another but will charge each one the full price if they don't know one another. A short conversation with other waiting passengers will do the trick!

28 43 02 23 12 | www.elysee-hotel.gr | Budget

SITÍA BEACH

This is the only large hotel in the region. It has three freshwater pools, a tennis court and a spa and fitness centre. The sea and beach is on the opposite side of the road (free beach towels for hotel guests) while the town centre and the bus terminal are only 5 minutes away. *161 rooms | Odós K. Karamanlí | tel. 28 43 02 88 21 | www. sitiabeach.com | Expensive*

INFORMATION

TOURIST INFORMATION
Leofóros Karamanlí/Odós Papandréou | tel. 28 41 02 42 00

WHERE TO GO

AGÍA FOTIÁ (151 E2–3) (𝄞 R4)

If you're in the mood for a little archaeological expedition, take the bus or a taxi to Agía Fotiá. In the fields below the village archaeologists have excavated an early Minoan cemetery with a large number of shaft graves and tomb chambers. A brown sign saying *Archaeological Site* shows the way. Continue about 250 m/820 ft on the dirt road until you reach the fenced-in excavation site on the low ▶INSIDER TIP◀ *Kouphóta hill* with ruins of an early Minoan settlement. As the beautifully prepared, EU-funded excavations are usually closed because of a shortage of attendants, you will have to look for a hole in the fence. On the way back to Sitía there is a small, bleak peninsula behind an old olive oil factory with the remains of the settlement of Trypitós from Hellenic times. There are no attendants there, either. *7 km/4.4 mi*

The countryside around Sitía in the east of Crete is full of peaceful olive groves

CHAMÉSI (150 C3) *(Q4)*

A spot for all those who love the beauty of simplicity: On a hilltop south-east of this traditional mountain village are the foundation walls of the only oval shaped *estate (admission free)* from Minoan times. You can enjoy a magnificent view across the land and sea from a field full of fennel, aromatic thyme, sage and oregano. To get there from the western end of the village, turn left beneath the remains of two windmills onto a dirt track that ends at the excavation site after about 700 m/2300 ft. *10 km/6.2 mi*

FANEROMÉNIS MONASTERY (151 D2) *(Q4)*

Fancy something unusual, but somehow typically Cretan? Then leave Sitía on the road to Iráklio, and after 2 km/1.2 mi turn right onto a narrow road signposted "Agion Panton Gorge". It ends after about 10 km/6.2 mi at a mini village that is inhabited in summer only for the wine harvest, and in winter for the olive harvest. However, the taverna (*Budget*) is usually open all year round – and usually without guests. The landlady is delighted whenever a guest does turn up – and no wonder, because otherwise she only has a few chickens to keep her company. Still, she always has supplies of fresh salad ingredients and vegetables. Just 50 steps from this unusual spot is a no less curious, long since abandoned, small monastery. Probably founded in the 15th century, it is boldly positioned over the gorge. You can see a few remains of 17th century frescoes in the sooty vaults of the church. Somehow, it goes perfectly with the general ghost town atmosphere that prevails. *10 km/6.2 mi*

INSIDER TIP ÍTANOS (151 F2) (*∅ R4*)

Bathing on the edge of the desert – that's what an hour on the beach at Ítanos feels like. Simple, small African-looking houses rise from the dunes. Even the sparse remains of an ancient town with two early Christian basilicas are scattered around it. From the ☀ sandy beach with its crystal clear waters, the view stretches as far as Cape Síderos, the north-eastern tip of Crete, which the military has unfortunately claimed for itself. No deckchairs on the beach and not a single hotel in sight for miles. Ítanos is a perfect alternative to the crowded, palm tree lined beach of Vái which is close by! *25 km/15.5 mi*

KÁTO ZÁKROS ★ (151 F4) (*∅ R5*)

It's a promise: it's going to be an entertaining day! If you're bathing on the miles-long shingle beach at Káto Zákros, remember there isn't a single piece of land between you and the coasts of Israel and Palestine about 850 km/530 mi away. That's vast. Káto Zákros itself consists of just a few little houses, loosely scattered over the coastal plain. It's hard to imagine anything more isolated. Just 10 minutes away, giant turtles sun themselves among the ruins of the 3500-year-old walls of a Minoan palace town *(Apr–Oct daily from 8am–6pm, Nov–Mar Tue–Sun 8am–3pm | admission 6 euros)* that once had 300 rooms – the eastern-

Dolce vita in Crete: eating in the shade on Káto Zákros beach

most one on Crete. From here, the Minoans travelled across the sea and traded with Egypt and other empires in the Near East. They also had a copper smelting furnace in Káto Zákros, the remains of which can still be seen here as one of the oldest industrial monuments in Europe. They were bold. But you don't really have to be bold today to enter the *Valley of the Dead*. Close to the palace, the path leads past a stream and up into the mountain village of *Zákros,* just a two-hour walk away. The first one-third of the path is the loveliest. You walk through a forest of oleanders that are taller than a man, and can see the numerous grottoes and caves in the reddish rock faces

where the Minoans and early Christians once buried their dead. You can stay if you like: INSIDER TIP *Stella's Apartments (tel. 28 43 02 37 39 | www.stelapts.com | Budget)* are part of a comfortably small bungalow development comprising 13 flats in a magical garden about 500 m/1640 ft from the beach in the midst of a rather desolate landscape. The tavern Platanákis *(daily from 10am | Budget)* located on the road next to the harbour serves particularly good food with a twist on the traditional Cretan cuisine. *45 km/28 mi*

INSIDER TIP MÓCHLOS
(150 B–C3) (ɰ P4)

You don't get to Móchlos by chance. There's nothing, absolutely nothing going on in the tiny village below the coastal road from Ágios Nikólaos to Sitía. Which is why you came here. To sit in the few tavernas by the water, bathe at the tiny beach – and perhaps go over to the uninhabited *islet* right off the coast, where American archaeologists are exposing a significant Minoan settlement. All life focuses on the platía by the water, with a spot of sand and several tavernas. If you haven't come to chill and read, you'll probably take a boat over to the island to see the excavations by the archaeologists of the University of North Carolina. The American archaeologist Richard Seager first broke the ground with spades here in 1908. The burial objects he excavated, including lovely gold jewellery, can now be seen in the museums at Iráklio, Agios Nikólaos and Sitía. Work on the excavations was resumed in 1990. Go to one of the tavernas and ask about *the boatman who is usually available from 1pm*. The only intact building on the island is the white *Chapel of St Nicolas*. Walk around the excavations, which have not yet been prepared for visitors, and you can look into several

Minoan graves, see the remains of Roman settlements – including fish tanks – and traces of a Byzantine settlement. It's not really particularly informative, but it's possibly wildly romantic. Warning: Better not to try to swim over to the island, as there are strong, unpredictable undercurrents. *30 km/18.6 mi*

NÉA PRESÓS (151 D3) (*∅ Q5*)

If you ever want to be all alone in an ancient town, climb up the hill that once bore the ancient Présos. A few sheep and goats will keep you company, but no travel groups or attendants far and wide. Nor is there much that is ancient, either, even though the hill was inhabited for 1500 years during the entire period of Greco-Roman Antiquity. What remained were the foundations of a temple, a house and a few stone blocks scattered about. What remains is the memory of a remote spot in the mountains, of pure nature. *Freely accessible | access road 2 km/1.2 mi, well signposted in the village of Néa Présos. 16 km/9.9 mi*

PALÉKASTRO (151 F2) (*∅ R4*)

The large inland village of Palékastro has been lucky. It is so far from the airport at Iráklio that the major international organisers are not interested in it because of the long transfer times – although it has some wonderful beaches. But this means that individual travellers remain amongst themselves. It's easy to get to the main beaches at Maridáki, Koureménos and Chióna, which are about 2–3 km/1–2 mi from the village square, on foot or by moped. There are several tiny bays to the south of Chióna Beach which are mainly nudist. Wind- and kitesurfers from all over the world meet on Koureménos Beach. The beach at *Chióna* has various excavations of a *Minoan town (Tue–Sun 8am–3pm |*

admission 2 euros) and three excellent tavernas. You will struggle to find a more idyllic setting on Crete than that provided by the two taverns located at the northern end of the beach. *Chióna (daily from noon | Expensive)* and *Bátis (daily from noon | Expensive)* both have terraces looking out over the sea towards the Middle East.

Sandwiched between the village and beach, you will find Olga in her tavern *Kakaviá (daily from 10am | Moderate)* who has been serving mainly Cretan guests for over 50 years with her fish soup (14 euros) according to an ancient secret recipe given to her by a fisherman. At the platía of Palékastro visit the restaurant *Hellas (daily from 8am | Budget)* which is traditional and unpretentious. At night it is the meeting place for locals and tourists alike. Blending well into the surrounding landscape is the hotel INSIDER TIP ▶ *Marína Village (tel. 28 43 06 12 84 | www.marina village.gr | Moderate)* with 32 rooms in several two-storey buildings in a garden with a pool. The beach and the town can each be reached by foot within 15 minutes. *24 km/14.9 mi*

THRIPTÍ (150 B4) (*∅ P5*)

Vines are cultivated here just below the 1476 m/4843 ft high *Afendís Kawússi* in a landscape which is reminiscent of the tea plantations in the Indian and Sri Lankan highlands. Vintners live here from summer until autumn and here Crete shows a very ancient side. You can reach Thriptí by a jeep via a forest road from *Káto Chorió* and from here you can drive across the mountains to *Orinó* with its many threshing floors and carob trees, through untouched mountain villages like *Skinokápsala* and *Ágios Jánnis*, to reach the southern coast at *Koutsounári*. *50 km/31.1 mi to Thriptí, 70 km/43.5 mi to the coast*

TÓPLOU MONASTERY (151 E2) *(𝔐 R4)*
Some Cretans believe that naughty boys reside in this monastery. That's because its few monks recently sold large sections of this still completely unspoilt north-eastern part of the island to multinational investors, who have plans to build Crete's largest luxury resort there, including several golf courses. Conservationists took the matter to the Supreme Court of Justice, but the monastery won. The landscape here may be "developed". Construction work has not yet commenced, so seize this opportunity to experience north-west Crete while it is still "under-developed". The fortress-like medieval monastery is the only building here far and wide, and is like an oasis in the midst of barren rocks and poor meadows. The *church* has one of Greece's loveliest icons with numerous figures. It was painted by one Johannes Kornáros in 1770, and illustrated in many miniature-like individual representations the text of a 7th century ode entitled, "Thou art all-powerful, oh Lord!". Not a few people wish it would produce a miracle round about now. *Daily 9am–1pm and 2–6pm | admission 3 euros. 21 km/13.1 mi*

VÁI ⭐ (151 F2) *(𝔐 R4)*
Of all the beaches on Crete, the one at Vái is the most overrated. The fine sand beach adjoins Crete's biggest palm tree grove, although no one is allowed to go there. It became world-famous when it was still without a fence. Every day during the summer, it now attracts more visitors than it can handle. The beach car park has become bigger than the beach itself. There are no hotels yet, but there are two *tavernas (daily from 9am | Budget), both of which belong –* yes, you've guessed it – to Tóplou Monastery. The water sports station also has to lease it premises from the monks. But de-

cide for yourself. If you find it all too awful for words, it won't take you long to get to the empty beaches like the ones at Ítanos, Palékastro and Káto Zákros. *25 km/15.5 mi*

XERÓKAMBOS ⭐ (151 E4) *(𝔐 R5)*
Despite having been accessible by tarmac roads for years, Xerókambos in the very south-east of the island is still a secret hideaway for people who prefer quiet beaches. There are many of them here: small hidden bays in the east and the 500 m/1640 ft long wide sandy *Ámbelos Beach* on the south coast. There are a few isolated tavernas and guest houses and no umbrellas to rent. Very reasonable with modern interiors and only 350 m/1150 ft from the next beach is the guesthouse *Liviko View (4 rooms | tel. 28 43 02 70 00 | www.livikoview.gr)* and adjoining taverna *(Budget)*. Between the beaches archaeologists have uncovered the ruins of a Hellenic settlement on a plateau next to a St Nicholas chapel. *43 km/26.7 mi*

We have to stay outside: shorts and naked shoulders are taboo in Tóplou

DISCOVERY TOURS

① CRETE AT A GLANCE

START: ① Iráklio
END: ① Iráklio

14 days
Driving time
(without stops)
30 hours

Distance:
🚗 1100 km/684 mi

COSTS: hire car from 400 euros, petrol approx. 150 euros, admission fees approx. 70 euros, boat trips approx. 30 euros, accommodation from approx. 550 euros/person

WHAT TO PACK: swim gear, sun protection, hiking boots

IMPORTANT TIPS: You can also start and end this tour at the airport in Chaniá.

Experience all the many facets of Crete on this tour. You'll visit the island's towns and its most significant excavation sites, drive over mountains and plateaus,

Would you like to explore the places that are unique to this island? Then the Discovery Tours are just the thing for you – they include terrific tips for stops worth making, breathtaking places to visit, selected restaurants and fun activities. It's even easier with the Touring App: download the tour with map and route to your smartphone using the QR Code on pages 2/3 or from the website address in the footer below – and you'll never get lost again even when you're offline.

→ p. 2/3

follow steep coastal cliffs and test the waters at different beaches. Along the way, you can meet Cretan farmers on village squares, ride a donkey, go water skiing and shop to your heart's content. And, if you're up for it, you can hop aboard a boat tour or hike through a canyon.

You won't have to tackle the heavy traffic in the island's capital because the motorway that begins at the airport of ❶ Iráklio → p. 58 will take you to the west in good time. During the first hour's drive, enjoy the views of the Aegean coast and the Psilorítis Mountains at a height of

DAY 1

❶ Iráklio

77 km/47.9 mi

❷ Réthimno
🏛 🍷 🍴 🛏

DAY 2
59 km/36.7 mi

❸ Chaniá
🏛 🏛 🍴 ⛵ 🖼 🎵
🛏

DAY 3
45 km/28 mi

❹ Polirrinía
🍴

8 km/5 mi

❺ Kissámos
🛏

DAY 4
42 km/26.1 mi

❻ Elafonísi
🏖 🍴

32 km/19.9 mi

❼ Paleochóra
🍴 🍸 🏰 ☀ 🛏

DAY 5
35 km/21.8 mi

❽ Agía Iríni
🌳 🥾

18 km/11.2 mi

❾ Soúgia
🏖 🛏

DAY 6
38 km/23.6 mi

❿ Samariá Gorge
🌳

27 km/16.8 mi

⓫ Fournés
🌳 🍴

50 km/31.1 mi

⓬ Georgioúpoli
🏖 🛏

DAY 7
15 km/9.3 mi

⓭ Chóra Sfakíon
☕

almost 2500 m/8200 ft. The first destination is ❷ **Ré-thimno → p. 46**. If you are in the mood for fresh fish in the evening, head to the taverna **Knossós** on the Venetian harbour for a romantic dinner. After exploring the town in the morning – make sure to visit the **folklore museum** – drive on to ❸ **Chaniá → p. 32** around midday. Check out the **nautical** and **archaeological museums** and inspect the replica of a **Minoan ship**. Stroll through the **market hall** and the leather shops on **Odós Skrídloff**. Around 6pm, hop aboard a boat at the pier near the Janissaries Mosque for an hour-long tour out on the water so that you can see how beautiful the city looks when it basks in the evening light with the White Mountains in the background. Later on, you might take a carriage ride through the romantic **old town** centre with its many shops. If you would like to listen to live Cretan lyra music, an almost certain bet is the taverna **Chalkína** because musicians play here almost every night. **On the third day, start off around 10am and head westward.** Explore the narrow paths around the isolated village of ❹ **Polirrinía → p. 44**. Eat lunch in the simple country-style taverna **Akrópolis** (*Budget*) and then check into a hotel near the beach in ❺ **Kissámos → p. 43**. **In the morning drive from the winding roads to the South-Seas-like lagoon of** ❻ **Elafonísi → p. 40** and, after a long swim and lunch, **take the same way back to just before Míli, then turn right and return via Strovlés, Drís, Pleme-neniá and Kakodíki to the south coast and** ❼ **Paleochóra → p. 43**, where in the evening, the main street seems to turn into one big open-air taverna. The best place to watch the beautiful sunset is from the walls of the **Kástro Sélino**.

Early the next morning, drive up through the White Mountains to the northeast. Park in ❽ **Agía Iríni → p. 43** at the upper end of the gorge of the same name and hike as far into it as you would like. Four hours is probably a good benchmark. When you're ready to seek out your hotel and take a swim, drive on to ❾ **Soúgia → p. 45** on the Libyan Sea. On the next day, you will come to the **Omalós Plateau** and you can take a look into the famous ❿ **Samariá Gorge → p. 116**. For a late lunch packed full of vitamins, stop at the **Botanical Park of Crete → p. 40** in ⓫ **Fournés**. **Quiet side roads will bring you through small mountain villages to the north coast and further on past Apterá to** ⓬ **Georgioúpoli → p. 41**, which is a good place to take an evening swim and spend the night. **In the morning, drive west on the motorway and then turn**

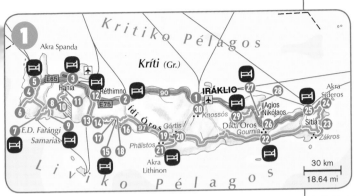

left to the south coast. Stop for at least a coffee at the old harbour of ⑬ **Chóra Sfakíon** → p. 40 and definitely go for an early afternoon swim at the sandy beach in front of the castle ⑭ **Frangokastéllo** → p. 41. Spend the next two nights in ⑮ **Plakiás** → p. 56. **On your first morning here, take a boat around 10am to the one-of-a-kind beach at** ⑯ **Préveli** → p. 57 with its groves of palm trees that you can explore along the dry paths or by wading through the stream. In the evening, you will have time to drive from Plakiás to the nearby mountain villages of ⑰ **Sellía** → p. 56 and ⑱ **Mýrthios** → p. 56 for a bit of shopping and a stroll. Have dinner in Myrthíos at the taverna **Panórama** (*Moderate*) with its fabulous view of the sea.

The next stretch of the tour focuses on interesting archaeological sites. In the morning, visit the palace of ⑲ **Festós** → p. 70 and the remains of the former Roman capital of ⑳ **Górtis** → p. 70. For some lunch and a swim, head for the beach of ㉑ **Mátala** → p. 69. Take in the atmosphere of this former Hippie haven and check in for the night. Take off early the next morning and drive as far as ㉒ **Ierápetra** → p. 85 on the eastern side of the island. Both the atmosphere and the climate here seem to resemble that of North Africa. Climb up to the top of the Venetian fortress for a sweeping view of the sea. **Start early on your 11th day, not later than 8am, and drive east to the Minoan palace of** ㉓ **Káto Zákros** → p. 98. Then drive on to the palm-tree studded beach of ㉔ **Vái** → p. 101, which has a good water sports centre, **before driving westward along the northern coast to the peaceful little rural town of** ㉕ **Sitía** → p. 93. For a fine dining experience and creative Cretan cuisine,

⑭ Frangokastéllo

26 km/15.2 mi

⑮ Plakiás

DAY 8

14 km/8.7 mi

⑯ Préveli

17 km/10.6 mi

⑰ Sellía

5 km/3.1 mi

⑱ Mýrthios

DAY 9

63 km/39.2 mi

⑲ Festós

16 km/9.9 mi

⑳ Górtis

23 km/14.3 mi

㉑ Mátala

DAY 10

121 km/75 mi

㉒ Ierápetra

DAY 11

85 km/52.8 mi

㉓ Káto Zákros

35 km/21.8 mi

㉔ Vái

24 km/14.9 mi

㉕ Sitía

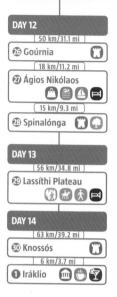

head to **The Balcony** restaurant in the old town centre. Afterwards, spend the night in one of the nice guest houses in town. Your goal for the next day is not only to explore the former Minoan town of 26 **Goúrnia** → p. 79, but also 27 **Ágios Nikólaos** → p. 72. It's a good place to do a little shopping and go for a swim, but you can also head to nearby Eloúnda to take a boat trip (about 3 hours) to the former lepers' island 28 **Spinalónga** → p. 83.

Your second to last full day is dedicated to rural tranquillity as you **drive past Neápoli and Zénia up to the** 29 **Lassíthi Plateau** → p. 80. Ride a donkey to the stalactite cave of Psychró, walk through the fields along the dirt paths and spend the night on the plateau. On the 14th day of your trip, spend the morning at the palace of 30 **Knossós** → p. 66 **and return to the island's capital** 1 **Iráklio** → p. 58 around midday. Definitely plan on spending about two hours in the **Archaeological Museum**, then INSIDER TIP perhaps jog 2 km/1.2 mi from the fortress Koúles along the harbour pier and take in the lively Cretan atmosphere in the cafés and tavernas one last time.

2 NATURE & HISTORY IN THE COUNTRYSIDE AROUND RÉTHIMNO

START: 1 Réthimno	1 day
END: 1 Réthimno	Driving time
Distance:	(without stops)
100 km/62 mi	2.5 hours

COSTS: admission fees approx. 6 euros/person, petrol approx. 15 euros

WHAT TO PACK: sturdy shoes, a torch, swim gear, picnic lunch

IMPORTANT TIPS: You can take a car or a motorcylce/motor scooter for this tour.

Despite the millions of holidaymakers who flock to Crete, there are still lots of small villages away from the coast in which it seems like time has stood still. This round-trip route will take you to several of them. There are no major activities on the agenda, as the plan is to quietly observe the locals as they go about their daily lives. You will also get a taste for the natural world of Greece's largest island in all its glory as you leave the crowds of tourists behind you on the coast.

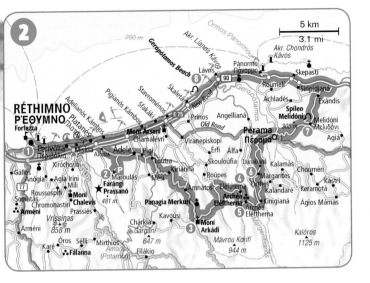

Enjoy a peaceful swim in Makrigialós at the long sandy beach and have a delightful lunch at the town's harbour.

08:00am Leave **①** Réthimno → p. 46 via the old coastal road that runs through the hotel quarter because there are no signs marking the improvised ramps on the motorway. In Plataniás, a well-marked road to Arkádi monastery branches off from the coastal road. Shortly before you reach Ádele, take a little detour to the old Venetian village of **②** Marulás. A good portion of the historic houses here have been bought by foreigners and extensively renovated. Walk around the village for about a half an hour and then drive back to the main road. **As the road climbs upward, it passes through several villages and then through a narrow valley.** Almost unexpectedly, you will finally come to the isolated **③** Arkádi Monastery → p. 55 high up on a plateau. You should plan on spending about an hour looking around the most significant of the Cretan national shrines.

The asphalt road leads from Arkádi Monastery towards Eléftherna. At first, it still crosses over the plateau, offering picture-perfect views of Arkádi and the surrounding area from different points along the way. Drive through the desolate and barren maquis landscape, past grazing

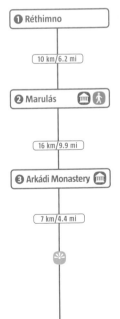

① Réthimno

10 km/6.2 mi

② Marulás 🏛 🚶

16 km/9.9 mi

③ Arkádi Monastery 🏛

7 km/4.4 mi

A fine performance: the cisterns at Archéa Eléftherna were hammered into the rock 2300 years ago

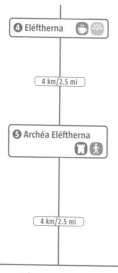

④ Eléftherna 🍴 🌼

4 km/2.5 mi

⑤ Archéa Eléftherna 🏛 🚶

4 km/2.5 mi

goats and sheep, **before taking the often empty road to the village of ④ Eléftherna**. There are four quaint coffee houses in which at least a few chatty older gentlemen always seem wait for new patrons to come in. The highest mountain on the island, Mount Psilorítis, can easily be seen from here. Eléftherna has about 250 permanent residents and sits at a height of 400 m/1310 ft.

As you drive on, you will come to the neighbouring village of ⑤ INSIDER TIP **Archéa Eléftherna**, which stands on the site of the significant ancient city of Eléftherna. Systematic excavations first began here in 1985. Every summer, researchers from the University of Crete continue to dig for artefacts. **The best thing to do is drive from the village square down to the taverna I Akropolis (*Budget*) and then set off on foot to explore the ancient ruins. A five-minute walk along the remains of the old city wall will bring you to two huge cisterns** that were hewed into the rock about 2300 years ago. You can explore them carefully if you have a torch. **If you continue along the path to the north, you will come to a terrace after about 6–7 minutes** that is home to the excavated ruins of a shrine of some kind beneath the old olive trees. This is the perfect place to enjoy a peaceful picnic to the natural music of the cicadas. You'll have to get back in the car to get to one of the other excavation areas of Eléftherna. **Follow the signs of the road to Margarítes that read "Ancient Eleftherna".** They will bring you to the remains of a Roman thermal bath and an early Christian Basilica.

01:00pm ⑥ **Margarítes → p. 55** is the name of the next destination, which you should reach around 1pm. **At the first potter's workshop on the right side of the road,** you can watch as man-sized storage vessels are made right before your eyes. The Cretans call them *pithoi*. A number of other local potters sell other clay creations that are easier to take home on a plane. The two **tavernas on the village** square of Margarítes are equally good and serve fantastic food. Other tavernas are located directly on the road at the lower end of the village. **The route continues downhill until you come to the old national road, which was the only link between Réthimno and Iráklio until the beginning of the 1980s. Turn right onto the national road in the direction of Pérama. When you get there, turn left towards the coast. You will rumble over a narrow bridge across a river that only flows in the winter and then turn right just after the bridge to head to** ⑦ **Melidóni**. Shortly before you reach the village, you can stop on the right-hand side at the olive **oil factory Paráskákis** and buy some good oil to take home. **From the village square, you should drive another 2–3 km/1.2–1.9 mi in the direction of Agía** because a number of charcoal kilns are fired here. Afterwards, the village square in Melidóni is a great place to take a break before driving up to the **stalactite cave of Melidóni → p. 55,** which is another Cretan national memorial site.

Depart Melidóni and drive to the sleepy hamlet of Exándis. Turn right onto the road leading uphill to get to the new national road, which you will then take to the west. If you feel like taking a swim as the sun sets over the Aegean, the long ⑧ **Geropótamos Beach** is the perfect spot. When it's time for dinner, head back to ① **Réthimno**.

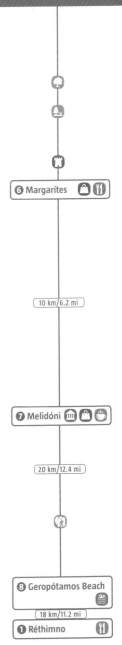

⑥ Margarítes

10 km/6.2 mi

⑦ Melidóni

20 km/12.4 mi

⑧ Geropótamos Beach

18 km/11.2 mi

① Réthimno

③ QUIET VILLAGES BETWEEN THE AEGEAN & LIBYAN SEAS

START: ① Sitía END: ① Sitía	1 day Driving time (without stops) 2 hours
Distance: 🚗 90 km/55.9 mi	

COSTS: approx. 50 euros for petrol and food & drink for 2 people
WHAT TO PACK: sturdy shoes, swim gear

IMPORTANT TIPS: You will need a car or a motorcycle/motor scooter for this tour.

Despite the millions of holidaymakers who flock to Crete, there are still lots of small villages away from the coast in which it seems like time has stood still. This round-trip route will take you to several of them. There are no major activities on the agenda, as the plan is to quietly observe the locals as they go about their daily lives. You will also get a taste for the natural world of Greece's largest island in all its glory as you leave the crowds of tourists behind you on the coast. Enjoy a peaceful swim in Makrigialós at the long sandy beach and have a delightful lunch at the town's harbour.

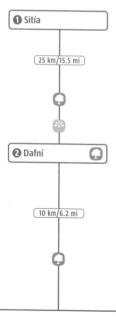

① Sitía

25 km/15.5 mi

② Dafní

10 km/6.2 mi

09:00am Depart ① Sitía → p. 93 and head south, following the signs for Ierápetra. As soon as you get to Piskokéfalo, **turn right onto the small road to Análipsi. After passing through Achládia, the road climbs up to the pass at Skordílo.** In early summer, gorse seems to bloom everywhere. Later in the season, it looks like the rocky landscape has been blanketed with puffy pillows of green herbs. At the top of the pass, you will get your first glimpse of the Libyan Sea. **Drive down into the high valley of ② Dafní**, which is full of olive trees. **After you've left Dafní, you will come to another mountain valley further below.** In this area, you will see blocks of pure chalk lying on the side of the road. Get your creative juices flowing and draw a little picture on the road with one of the small pieces of chalk lying around. As you drive on, you will come to the mouth of a valley that runs from the north coast into the mountains. Storms often blow through this natural wind channel, shearing through the pine trees. Over the next few miles, you'll notice how the winds have cut the most bizarre, lopsided shapes into the trees. **Drive through Chrisopigí and pass by the totally isolated mountain village of Lápithos and make your next**

stop in ❸ **Stavrochóri**. The particularly quaint Kafenío on the through road is the perfect place for a long overdue coffee! **The road ends after another 35 km/21.8 mi in the coastal village of ❹ Koutsourás**. Greenhouses have been built here right in the centre of the village – take a minute to inspect one of them up close!

02:00pm Take the coastal road to the left and drive for just five minutes to ❺ **Makrígialos** → p. 90. After a swim in the Libyan Sea, INSIDERTIP the small harbour is an excellent place to grab lunch. Then, follow the main road again. Just after Vóri, turn right and drive up to ❻ **Etiá** and the village of ❼ **Chandrás**. On this elevated

❸ **Stavrochóri**		☕
7 km/4.4 mi		
❹ **Koutsourás**		
3 km/1.9 mi		
❺ **Makrígialos**	🏖	🍴
17 km/10.6 mi		
❻ **Etiá**		☕
3 km/1.9 mi		
❼ **Chandrás**		☕

6 km/3.7 mi

8 Néa Presós

18 km/11.2 mi

1 Sitía

plateau where sultanas are the main crop, the pace of life is leisurely and the tourists are few as you'll easily notice in the village Kafenía. Once you are ready to leave this tranquillity behind, take a small detour from **8 Néa Presós → p. 100** to the meagre ruins of the ancient city of Pressós on a hill. You can hike along the narrow paths with the most beautiful views of the Cretan Mountains to your heart's content. Late in the afternoon, **drive north** to get back to **1 Sitía**.

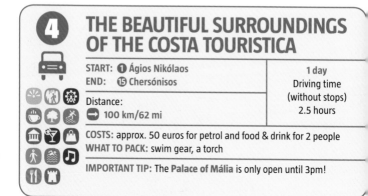

4 THE BEAUTIFUL SURROUNDINGS OF THE COSTA TOURISTICA

START: **1 Ágios Nikólaos**	1 day
END: **15 Chersónisos**	Driving time (without stops)
Distance:	2.5 hours
➡ 100 km/62 mi	

COSTS: approx. 50 euros for petrol and food & drink for 2 people
WHAT TO PACK: swim gear, a torch

IMPORTANT TIP: The **Palace of Mália** is only open until 3pm!

Most of the large hotels on Crete are located between Ágios Nikólaos and Chersónisos as the herds of tourists flock to this stretch of the coast. But, if you go just a few miles away from the beaches, you can still get a taste of the real Crete. Although this tour passes through the major resort towns, it also explores the untouched nature, lively village squares, monasteries and good tavernas that make for an authentic Cretan experience. You'll also have plenty of time for a swim as well as a short adrenaline rush from a bungee jump or water sports adventure.

1 Ágios Nikólaos

20 km/12.4 mi

2 Vroúchas

4 km/2.5 mi

3 Káto Loúmas

3 km/1.9 mi

4 Skiniás

6 km/3.7 mi

5 Karídi

08:00am Follow the coastal road from **1 Ágios Nikólaos → p. 72 northwards to Eloúnda and Pláka. Leave the coast behind and drive up to the mountain village of 2 Vroúchas**. Enjoy the spectacular view of the fortress island of Kalidón and Spinalónga **→ p. 83**. Keep driving through the countryside dotted with isolated small villages such as **3 Káto Loúmas** and **4 Skiniás**. If you find an open Kafenío, stop inside – the locals will be surprised to see a tourist. **At the fork just after leaving Váltos, take the road to 5 Karídi**. Shortly before you get to the village, you will spy a road to the left leading to the **Aréti Monastery** at a height of 530 m/1739 ft, which is worth

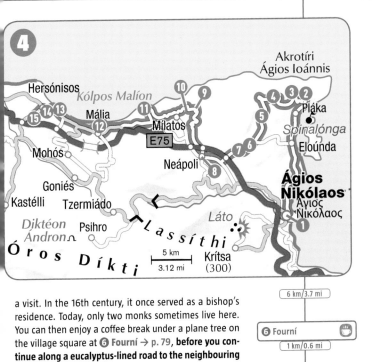

a visit. In the 16th century, it once served as a bishop's residence. Today, only two monks sometimes live here. You can then enjoy a coffee break under a plane tree on the village square at ⑥ Fourní → p. 79, **before you continue along a eucalyptus-lined road to the neighbouring**

6 km/3.7 mi

⑥ Fourní

1 km/0.6 mi

Stop for coffee in the lovely village of Fourní nestled between the mountains

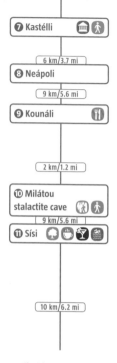

7 Kastélli	🏛️ 🚶
6 km/3.7 mi	
8 Neápoli	
9 km/5.6 mi	
9 Kounáli	🍴
2 km/1.2 mi	
10 Milátou stalactite cave	👥 🚶
9 km/5.6 mi	
11 Sísi	🍹 🍔 🍷 🏖️
10 km/6.2 mi	

village of **7 Kastélli** → p. 79. Spend a quarter of an hour strolling through the pretty village, which has numerous Venetian buildings.

01:00pm Drive through Nikithianó to **8 Neápoli**, and then follow the signs to Iráklio in order to get to Latsída. In the centre of the village, turn right and then just outside the village, turn left towards **9 Kounáli**. Stop for an excellent lunch along the main road on the shady terrace of the taverna **To Kounáli** (*Budget*) owned by a former ship's cook and his flower-crazy daughter. A bit of exercise will do you good after your meal. **On the curvy road between Kounáli and Mílatos, park your car and take a short walk to the 10 Milátou stalactite cave** on the left-hand side. Don't forget a torch! After exploring this subterranean world, **drive through Mílatos to arrive at 11 Sísi** → p. 82 with its amazingly beautiful, although extremely short, fjord. For a cup of coffee or a refreshing drink, head to the **Skipper Cocktail Bar** directly above the fjord. If you feel like testing the water, there is a small sandy beach on the western end of the fjord where you can go for a swim.

As you leave Sísi, follow the signs for Mália and Iráklio, which will bring you to the motorway. After about 2 km/1.2 mi, follow the signs to the Minoan Palace

The Minoans not only built a palace at a prime location in Knossós, but also in Mália

of Mál**ia** → p. 67. If you get there before it closes, it's worth taking a look. If you're too late, you'll have to make do with a glimpse through the barbed wire fence. You haven't wasted your time either way as the lovely beach and harbour of ⑫ **Málía** → p. 67 are just a stone's throw away. **If you walk 150 m/490 ft to the west**, you can play a INSIDER TIP round of backgammon, Uno or Scrabble with Greek letters at the **Snack Bar Blue Sea** (*Budget*). **Afterwards, continue to the west on the old national road (avoid the motorway!) until you come to the resort of Stalída on the eastern edge of ⑬ Limé-nas Chersónisou** → p. 65. It is home to the **Star Beach Water Park** → p. 124 with its bungee crane and a variety of water sports stations. How about a little parasailing adventure?

08:30pm **Drive into the town of Liménas Chersónisou and follow the signs for the village of ⑭ Koutouloufári, about half a mile above the main town**, where plenty of jewellery and handicrafts are on offer. For a late dinner, head to the village square of ⑮ **Chersónisos** → p. 65. Every Monday, a folklorist "Cretan Evening" is held here.

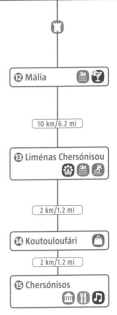

⑫ Málía

10 km/6.2 mi

⑬ Liménas Chersónisou

2 km/1.2 mi

⑭ Koutouloufári

2 km/1.2 mi

⑮ Chersónisos

---

5 A SELF-GUIDED HIKE THROUGH CRETE'S MOST FAMOUS GORGE

START: ❶ Chaniá	2 days
END: ❶ Chaniá	Hiking time
Distance:	difficulty:	(without stops)
📅 150 km/93 mi	▫️ medium	5–6 hours

COSTS: bus tickets approx. 20 euros, accommodation/breakfast approx. 50 euros/double room, admission (gorge) 5 euros, boat trip Agía Roúmeli – Chóra Sfakíon 12.70 euros
WHAT TO PACK: hiking shoes, water, sun protection, swim gear, blister care kit

IMPORTANT TIPS: The gorge is only accessible from the beginning of May to 15 October.
The last public bus from Chaniá departs at 8.45am.
Bus timetables on *www.e-ktel.com*; ship timetables on *www.anendyk.gr*
Hotels on the Ómalos plateau: Exári (*www.exari.gr*) or Néos Ómalos (*www.neos-omalos.gr*)

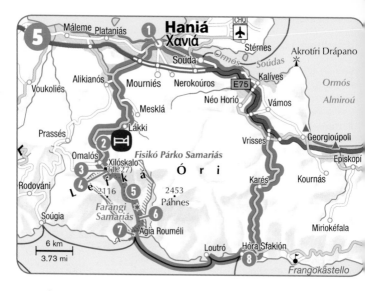

The ★ Samariá gorge in the White Mountains of western Crete is one of the longest and deepest in Europe at a length of 18 km/11.2 mi. The vertical rock walls are up to 600 m/1970 ft high, and at its narrowest point, the Iron Gate, the gorge is only a few meters wide. If you want to avoid the tourist crowds, you should head up INSIDERTIP early on the day before you actually plan to hike.

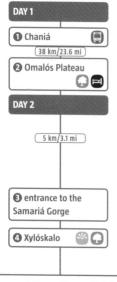

DAY 1

❶ Chaniá 🚌

38 km/23.6 mi

❷ Omalós Plateau 🏡🛏

DAY 2

5 km/3.1 mi

❸ entrance to the Samariá Gorge

❹ Xylóskalo ❄🏡

08:45am Make sure to be on-time to catch the bus from ❶ Chaniá → p. 32 up to the ❷ Omalós Plateau because there is no later bus. You will arrive around 10.30am and then treat yourself to a refreshing day of relaxation at a height of over 1000 m/3280 ft. Spend the night in the tranquil village of **Omalós**.

07:00am Start off on your hike through the gorge when it opens early the next morning at 7am. This way, you won't have to cross through the last part of the trail between the exit of the gorge and the Libyan Sea, where there is no shade, in the midday heat. **But first, you will have to walk about 5 km/3.1 mi from your hotel in Ómalos along an asphalt road, unless your hotelier organizes rides, to the ❸ entrance of the Samariá Gorge. The actual trail begins a few steps further at a height of 1229 m/4032 ft at the ❹ Xylóskalo, the wooden steps that bring you into the gorge.** Don't worry, though, because these are not actually stairs, but rather a pleasant forest path with steps here and there. Under the eyes of the Gíngilos (2080 m/6820 ft), the trail wanders for **about an hour up through the forest to the floor of the gorge** through which a rushing stream flows. You will come to the abandoned village of ❺ Samariá, which has a fresh water spring, a first-aid station and toilets. The last residents left in 1962 when the gorge was turned into a national park.

As the trail continues, the gorge narrows steadily until you come to the so-called ❻ Iron Gate (Sideróporta), where it is only 3–4 m/10–13 ft wide. **Shortly thereafter, the coastal plain will appear before you, and then it is just another 3 km/1.9 mi (without any shade) to the coastal hamlet of ❼ Agía Rouméli** with its many tavernas, guest houses and a long pebble beach. The first thing you should do is buy your tickets for the ferry to Chóra Sfakíon. Then you can enjoy a long break in one of the tavernas and maybe a swim. **The last ferry usually leaves around 5.30pm, arriving at its destination about an hour later.** In ❽ Chóra Sfakíon → p. 40, the public buses to Chaniá always wait for the ferry to dock. You should arrive back in ❶ Chaniá around 8.30pm.

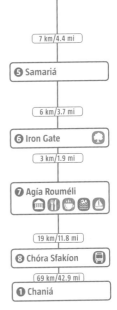

7 km/4.4 mi

❺ Samariá

6 km/3.7 mi

❻ Iron Gate

3 km/1.9 mi

❼ Agía Rouméli

19 km/11.8 mi

❽ Chóra Sfakíon

69 km/42.9 mi

❶ Chaniá

Sparkling companion: a stream flanks your path at the foot of the gorge

SPORTS & ACTIVITIES

The mountains and sea are the island's sports arenas. Daredevils try their luck on Europe's second highest bungee jump, the more cautious venture out on an SUP board for some yoga. Some like to attach themselves to a parachute and be pulled over the water, while cyclists can choose between mountain bikes, racing bikes and e-bikes.

BUNGEE JUMPING

A INSIDER TIP bungee jump at Arádena, near the south coast takes bravery. You can dive 138 m/453 ft from the bridge into the Arádena Gorge: *Liquidbungy (July–Aug Sat/Sun from noon | 100 euros | Arádena | mobile phone 69 37 61 51 91 | www.bungy.gr).* There is also the option of a more moderate drop from a crane by the sea at the water resort *Star Beach* at Chersónisos on the eastern edge of the town. The drop is only 50 m/164 ft which also allows for tandem jumps: *Star Beach Bungee (daily from 10am | approx. 60 euros | Chersónisos | www. starbeach.gr).*

CLIMBING

The INSIDER TIP Asterússia Mountains on the south coast are an as-yet unknown El Dorado for climbers. The central place for them is the village of *Kapetaniraná*, where the contacts are Gunnar and Luisa Schuschnigg from Carinthia at

From the sedate to the spectacular: mountainbiking and hiking enthusiasts will be spoiled for choice

Korifi Tours (tel. 28 93 04 14 40 | www. korifi.de). For comprehensive information on the various areas there and elsewhere on Crete, contact *www.climbincrete.com*.

DANCING LESSONS

Have you been infected by "Zorba the Greek"? Then get yourself over to the south coast and Swiss-born Isabella Müllenbach at the *Haus Kavoúri (tel. 69 76 01 17 33 | www.housekavouri.com)*. She gives weekly lessons in Greek danc-

ing in Soúda at Plakiás, and you can also join in a few sessions on the spur of the moment.

DIVING

Cretan diving sites are particularly suited to beginners due to their crystal clear water, good centres and interesting underwater rock formations. However, there are few fish to be seen. In Crete archaeologists also have a say in the choice of dive sites as they fear that divers will disturb excavations and even smuggle pieces out of the country. A few diving schools (some also offer introductory courses for adults and for children):

– ● *Atlantis Diving Centre (Rithimna Beach | Ádele)* and in the *Grecotel Club Marine Palace (Panórmo | tel. 28 31 07 16 40 | www.atlantis-creta.com)*

– *Creta Maris Dive Center (Liménas Chersónisou | Hotel Creta Maris |tel. 28 97 02 21 22 | www.dive-cretamaris.gr)*

– *Dive Together (on the coastal road | Plakiás | tel. 28 32 03 23 13 | www.dive2gether.com)*

– *Notos Mare (at the new harbour | Chóra Sfakíon | tel. 28 25 09 13 33 | www.notosmare.com)*

HIKING

The E4 European long distance hiking trail stretches from the west to the east coast of Crete. You should allow at least four weeks for the complete hike. The signposting is good but not perfect. Fitness is essential because you will be crossing mountains and a tent would also be useful *(www.oreivatein.com)*.

You can also undertake many hikes on Crete on your own or book one or two-week hikes through specialist travel agencies at home or in Crete, like *Happy Walker (Odós Tombázi 56 | Réthimno | tel. 28 31 05 29 20 | www.happywalker.com)*.

HORSE RIDING

Riding stables for experienced riders are at the *Horsefarm Melanoúri* in Pitsídia *(tel. 28 92 04 50 40 | www.melanouri.com)* and the *Odysseia Stables (tel. 28 97 05 10 80, mobile phone 69 42 83 60 83 | www.horseriding.gr)* in Avdoú en route to the Lassíthi Plateau. Both offer accommodation as well.

MOUNTAIN BIKING

Crete is an ideal destination for mountain bikers. There are lots of good biking centres that offer a range of tour packages for all levels of difficulty. Those who prefer to take it easy can take a support van up to the starting point and then cycle downhill while ambitious bikers can challenge themselves cycling between mountain peaks. Organisers offer day trips (40–60 euros, children 25–40 euros) and week packages. E-bikes are mostly available, too.

Good agencies are *Adventurebikes (on the road from the platía to the beach | tel. 69 37 90 42 51)* in Georgioúpoli; Freak Mountainbike Centre *(mobile phone 69 85 81 02 40 | www.freakmountainbike.com)* in Palékastro; *Hellas Bike (main road opposite the Bank of Cyprus | tel. 28 21 06 08 58 | www.hellasbike.net)* in Agía Marína near Chaniá; *Olympic Bike (Adelianós Kámbos 32 | tel. 28 31 07 27 83 | www.olympicbike.com)* on the coastal road east of Réthimno and *Anso Travel (tel. 28 32 03 17 12 | www.ansovillas.com)* in Plakiás on the south coast.

There are six stations in *Crete Cycling (tel. on Crete 69 86 92 77 06 | www.crete-cycling.com)* in Eloúnda, Mália, Móchlos, Palékastro and Iráklio (all year), and Agía Galíni (which also has racing bikes). A good bike costs 13–22 euros a day or 80–115 euros per week. You can bring your own helmet and pedals. Challenging INSIDERTIP day trips on e-mountain bikes in very small groups are arranged by *Adam Frogákis (tel. 69 44 74 06 93 | www.adams-ebikes-crete.com)*. After being collected from the hotel between Iráklio and Sisi, it's off to the multilingual guide's home for an extensive breakfast.

SAILING

With an experienced skipper of Pélagos Diving Centre (*tel. 28 41 02 43 76/ www.sailcrete.com*) on board you can go sailing on a private yacht from Ági-

in kite surfing. The specialist in stand-up paddling (SUP) is the Cretan *Stéfanos Averkiou (Station Akrotíri peninsula, Loutráki, on the beach by the Mare Nostrum Villas | tel. 69 45 50 09 39 | www. supincrete.com)* from Chaniá. His offer

Beach life of the moving kind at Liménas Chersónisou

os Nikólaos to the islands of Spinalónga or Móchlos. From Ierápetra you can sail to the island of Chrisí *with Nautilos (Odós Markopoúlou 1 | mobile phone 69 72 89 42 79 | www.nautiloscruises.gr)*. You are welcome to lend a hand but it is not necessary. Multiple day trips with different destinations can also be arranged.

WATER SPORTS

Almost all the popular beaches offer water sports options, from water skiing to jet skiing and parasailing. Paddle boats and canoes can also be hired in front of the larger hotels and surfboards are available on many of the beaches. Good surf schools can be found at the larger centres like *Freak Station (tel. 69 79 25 38 61 | in the winter +43 6 88 64 81 10 04 | www.freak-surf.com)* on *Kuereménos beach* in Palékastro, who also specialise

includes hire, courses and guided day trips, and yoga on a paddleboard is his speciality.

WELLNESS & YOGA

Many luxury hotels have spas that are also open to non-residents. Particularly original is the tiny INSIDER TIP *Al Hammam (daily from 11am | Pl. El. Venizélou 14 | tel. 28 21 05 90 00 05)* on the Venetian harbour of Chaniá. It appears to have escaped from the atmosphere of past centuries, but is quite modern. You'll feel as if you were staying in a sultan's palace – just freer. ● Magical earth forces may be felt by yoga and t'ai chi practitioners and people attending meditational courses on the southern coast between Ágios Pávlos (145 E6) (*ɯ G5*) and Soúda (145 D5) (*ɯ F4*). More information: *www.yogaplus.co.uk*

TRAVEL WITH KIDS

On Crete little ones are welcome to be a part of life until well after midnight, even in the cafés and tavernas.

There aren't many special attractions for children, and playgrounds are often carelessly designed. Children's menus are only handed out in the tourist establishments. Instead, children are given a plate and take food from the adults's plates. Baby food and nappies are available in all supermarkets, and there are reduced bus fares for kids up to 12 years on scheduled buses and boat trips.

CHANIÁ

LIMNOÚPOLIS (143 E3) *(∅ C2)*

It's going to be an expensive day – parents and two children will have to part with at least 130 euros at this leisure pool. Not bothered? Then enjoy the five water slides (up to 55 metres high), Crazy and Lazy River and pools for all ages as often as you like. It is better to bring your own water with you, because the prices for drinks at the park are exorbitant. *End of \May-Oct daily from 10am-6pm | admission until 3pm 25 euros, 18 euros for children (4–12 years), and 17 euros or 14 euros from 3pm | Scheduled buses from Platía 1866 | Fun Train from Plataniás | www.limnoupolis.gr*

TAKE A CARRIAGE THROUGH THE TOWN (143 E3) *(∅ D2)*

Steady there now! In the harbour at Chaniá there are always horse-drawn carriages waiting for customers. Who

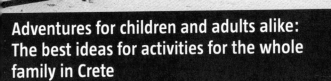

Adventures for children and adults alike: The best ideas for activities for the whole family in Crete

would like to join the driver on his seat? And how long would you like? The choice is 20 or 50 minutes *(15 or 45 euros). Twilight and early evening are the nicest times. Departure from the Janissaries Mosque*

INSIDER TIP **VENETIAN MODEL** (143 E3) (*D2*)

Children do not always have a lot to do at archaeological ruins. But once they have seen the model of the Venetian arsenal in the Nautical Museum in Chaniá they might look at other ruins differently and be able to imagine the galleys and ship docks coming to life in the empty ruins. *Mon–Fri 9am–6pm, Sat/Sun 10am–6pm, in the winter Mon–Sat 9am–4pm | entrance fee 3 euros, children (6–17 years) 2 euros | Aktí Kundurióti | Chaniá*

RÉTHIMNO

BARBAROSSA (145 D–E3) (*F3*)

Have Lego pirates taken over your bedroom at home? Then it's high time to treat your children to a trip on the pirate's ship. Of course, the crew consists of well fitted-out pirates who play and pose for photos with little ones – who are, of course, welcome to paint themselves accordingly. The tours take 1–3 hours. *Ticket 12–24 euros (for children as well) | from the Venetian harbour | www.dolphin-cruises.com*

TAKE A MINI TRAIN

Puffa puff – here comes the train! And although it's not a full-sized one that rolls along proper tracks on Crete, it is a motorised ● engine with three open carriages that rides along many of the streets on rubber tyres. The train timetable in Georgioúpoli is especially comprehensive. The trains don't just go to the beach hotels, but to the Kournás mountain lake with its beach and pedalos, or up into the lovely mountain village of *Argiroúpoli* (see page 53) where children are allowed to play in the waterfalls. There is also a guide for adults who provides lots of information. *Tours daily | 8–15 euros (for children as well)*

IRÁKLIO

CRETAQUARIUM ● (148 B2) (*ω L3*)

Have your children never seen an aquarium? Then you'll love this one. There are 32 pools on an old military barracks near Goúrnes with over 4000 marine residents. *May–Sep daily from 9.30am-9pm, otherwise until 5pm | admission 9 euros, 4 euros from Nov–Apr, children (5–17 years) 6 euros | www.cretaquarium.gr*

DINOSAUR PARK (148 B2) (*ω L3*)

There are no living dinosaurs to see on Crete, but the show in Goúrnes is extremely well-presented. You'll see 50 types of dinosaur on 4 acres, moving in 3D on the screen. There's even a dino-saur hospital with obstetrics ward to follow. *May–Sep. daily from 10am-8pm, Nov–Apr Sat/Sun 10am–5pm | admission 19 euros, children (4–12 years), 8 euros, cinema 5/3 euros extra | www.dinosauriapark.com*

DONKEY RIDES (148 C3) (*ω M4*)

Are your children old enough to ride? Then they'll enjoy riding on a donkey. You hardly see these grey animals any more in daily life on Crete; they have been replaced by tractors and pickups. But Manólis and his Swedish wife Karin still use them. Children and lightweight adults can climb into the saddle at INSIDERTIP ▶ *Kríti Farm (ride 12 euros for about 45 minutes, tour in a horse-drawn cart 15 euros | below the road from Chersónisos to the Lassíthi Plateau just past Potamiés | tel. 28 97 05 15 46).* Alternatively, you can also enjoy a half-hour ride in a horse drawn cart. The farm also has a rustic ranch-style *taverna (Budget)* and a small petting zoo – you can easily spend several hours here.

WATER PARKS

Bad luck! In Liménas Chersónisos there's now far too little beach for far too many people, which is why the two leisure pools are so well visited. The ● *Star Beach Water Park* (148 C2) (*ω M3*) *(daily 9am–7pm | admission free | on the coastal road at the eastern edge of Liménas Chersónisou)* east of Liménas with its loud music is more focused on the youth and disco lovers. The *Acqua Plus* (148 B2) (*ω M4*) *(daily 10am–7pm | entrance fee up to 24 euros, children (5–11 years) 16 euros, large discounts if you book online | 5 km/3.1 mi inland on the road to Kastélli | www.acquaplus.gr)* is a better option for families. Here you will find giant slides and lots of space to play. The park has transfer buses from Iráklio

„Mummy, what's that fish?" Not sure? You'll find the answer in the Cretaquarium

and other coastal resorts. Information available at any hotel on the island.

IERÁPETRA

INSIDER TIP **PLAY ROBINSON CRUSOE**
(150 A6) (*Ⓜ O7*)

Excursion boats to the uninhabited island of Chrisí leave from Ierápetra daily. If you arrange it with the captain you can even have an adventure and stay overnight and camp on the beach. In the summer you don't even need a tent. You can take provisions with you but there are also two tavernas on the island. Take a torch along.

SITÍA

WALK THROUGH THE "VALLEY OF THE DEAD" (151 E–F 3–4) (*Ⓜ R5*)

Do your children love spooky stories and adventures? Then why not take them on an easy 2-hour hike around the far east of the island. It starts in the mountain village of Zákros, and ends on the beach at Káto Zákros. For a good hour, you'll keep crossing a tiny mountain brook, sometimes on wobbly stones, sometimes on uprooted tree roots.

The Minoans buried their dead in the many caves in the canyon walls; it's up to you to make up the appropriate stories. At the end of the stream's valley, the oleander grows so tall and so densely it's a great place to play labyrinth or hide-and-seek. At the *Minoan Palace of Káto Zákros* you can observe lots of large terrapins sunning themselves on the large, ancient stone blocks – and right at the end bathe on the long gravel beach. The public bus will take you back to your car in Káto Zákros at the end.

FESTIVALS & EVENTS

The Cretans like to celebrate and a lot of the occasions for celebration are the various patron saint days. These village festivals usually start on the eve of the actual feast day with music and dancing. On the day of the festival itself there is often just a church service. Shrove Monday, Good Friday, Easter and Whitsun in the Greek Orthodox Church are celebrated according to the Julian calendar and rarely fall on our holy days.

During the summer, there are many music and cultural festivals in the towns. Apart from folklore, they focus more and more on modern Greek rock music. The programmes are unfortunately only published just before the event. Sometimes you can find them on the internet a few days in advance on *www.cultureguide.gr*.

FESTIVALS & EVENTS

CARNIVAL SUNDAY
Large carnival procession through the main roads of Réthimno with thousands dressed in costumes, lots of themed floats and loud samba music with Greek lyrics.

25 MARCH
Independence day. Schoolchildren often wear traditional costumes for the parades.

EASTER FRIDAY
Processions in all the towns and villages (from about 9pm)

EASTER SATURDAY
Easter mass from 11pm where almost all Cretans go. Fireworks shortly after midnight

SUNDAY AFTER EASTER
Church service in the cave at Mílatos followed by free entertainment and refreshments on the village square by the sea

MAY/JUNE
At Whitsun there are three days of open-air festivals in Mátala at the ● *Matala Beach Festival*.

JULY–SEPTEMBER
INSIDER TIP *Renaissance festival in Réthimno:* The festival with the most ambitious programme in Crete, offering talks, theatre and concerts paying homage to the Renaissance when the town prospered. The preferred place for events

Church fairs and processions: Crete's holiday calendar is defined by the Greek Orthodox holidays

is the amphitheatre in the Fortézza of Réthimno (12 days end of August/ beginning of September). *www.rfr.gr*
Cultural festival in Iráklio with many events at different places in the city. *www.heraklion.gr*

AUGUST

Community festival in Anógia with *lýra* competitions, singing and Cretan dancing (beginning of August)
Parish festivals with lots of music and dancing as well as festivals in town squares in almost all Cretan villages (14/15 Aug)
Potato festival in Tzermiádo on the Lassíthi Plateau with music, dancing, fair and free potato tasting (weekend after the 15th of Aug)
⚫ *Houdétsi Festival* at Iráklio: four-day festival of Cretan music with renowned interpreters. Admission is free, free transfer from Péza. *www.cretetravel.com/event/houdetsi-festival/*

OCTOBER

Parish festival at the Guvernétu Monastery near Chaniá with a procession from the monastery to the cave for a festive service (7 Oct)

PUBLIC HOLIDAYS

1 Jan	New Year's Day
6 Jan	Epiphany
25 March	Independence Day
19 Feb 2018, 26 April 2019	
	Shrove Monday
6 April 2018, 26 April 2019	
	Good Friday
8/9 April 2018, 28/29 April 2019	
	Easter
1 May	Labour Day
27/28 May 2018, 16/17 June 2019	
	Whitsun
15 Aug	Assumption Day
28 Oct	National holiday
25/26 Dec	Christmas

LINKS, BLOGS, APPS & MORE

www.explorecrete.com comprehensive website full of tourist information, with local news, maps and climate charts

www.incrediblecrete.gr beautifully designed website with lots of well-organised information on Crete's history, nature, hotels, alternative tourism and much more

www.crete.gr a website with information on the island's history, climate and environmental issues as well as what to do and where to eat

www.cretetravel.com hand-picked hotels, activities and travel tips

www.greecetravel.com/crete Matt Barrett, who knows his way around Greece since 1968, shares his personal tips about Crete, from taxis to food

www.we-love-crete.com web journal with much information on independent travel in Crete

www.cretegazette.com an on-line newspaper for Crete's English community with local news and articles about everyday events in Crete

www.completely-crete.com set up by two UK expats in order to share their insider knowledge about Crete

livingincrete-carolina.blogspot.com blog about Crete, which is especially good on news that could be interesting for tourists: new flight routes, new films about Greece, events and more

Regardless of whether you are still preparing your trip or already on Crete: these addresses will provide you with more information, videos and networks to make your holiday even more enjoyable

VIDEOS & MUSIC

www.cretetv.gr with the live stream of local TV station Kriti TV, you can follow the local news

www.explorecrete.com/videos/crete-videos.html a wide selection of good quality videos showcasing Cretan villages, beaches, archaeological sites as well as cultural videos about music, dance and Crete's traditions

vimeo.com/incrediblecrete beautifully made, sensuous short films that make you want to go to Crete on the spot!

APPS

Save Minotaur! You have to make your way through the labyrinth to save the Minotaur. The game has different levels of difficulty to suit all ages

Crete Street Map Load this onto your iPhone and have instant access to the island's city streets even when you have no internet access. Helpful: places like museums, banks or rental car stations are shown. You can also save your own places – for example, to remember where you parked your car...

Myths of Crete & Pre-Hellenic For those interested in the history and myths of Crete this app forms part of the e-book by Donald A Mackenzie. The app is for iPhones.

Cretan Beaches Descriptions, pictures and ratings of over 300 beaches everywhere on Crete

My Crete Guide Best-rated travel app for Crete, with (offline) maps, navigator and many tips on sights (also lesser known ones). Personalised information, weather, over 40 categories and info about the E4 hiking trail. For Android, free

TRAVEL TIPS

ARRIVAL

✈ There are daily flights to Crete all year with Olympic Air/Aegean Airlines (www.aegeanair.com) and Astra Airlines (www.astra-airlines.gr) via Athens or Thessaloniki. Between Easter and October there are also many direct charter and budget flights directly to Iráklio and Chaniá but these can sometimes be more expensive than normal flights. Flights from London to Iráklio take about 3 and a half hours and from Athens about 40 minutes. At both airports there are taxis for further transport. At Chaniá and Iráklio there are also reasonably priced buses to the nearby city centre. Crete's third biggest airport in Sitía in eastern Crete sees domestic flights from Astra Airlines and Sky Express (www.skyexpress.gr). Taxis are available at the arrival zone of the airport.

🛳 There is no direct ferry service from Italy. You have to cross to Patras on the Peloponnese first, then from Piraeus to Crete. Daily ferries to Chaniá and Iráklio (6–12 hours), several times a week to Réthimno and Sitía. In addition two or three times a week from Kissámos to the Peloponnese.

BANKS & MONEY

Bank opening hours are Mon–Thu 8am–2pm, Fri 8am–1.30pm. You can withdraw money from many cash machines with your credit or debit card.

BUS

There are regular – and cheap – public buses to almost every town in Crete and travelling by bus is recommended, since parking spaces are scarce. The blue buses only travel within municipal districts. Long distance buses (often green) travel between Iráklio, Ágios Nikólaos, Chaniá, Ierápetra, Sitía and Réthimno. Tickets are bought in advance at the bus terminals in the cities; if you get on later, you buy the tickets from the driver. Tickets for city buses can be bought at kiosks, hotel receptions and shops.

Timetables for western Crete can be found at: www.e-ktel.com, for eastern Crete at: www.ktelherlas.gr

CAMPING

Camping anywhere else but in a camp site is prohibited in Crete but is often done on isolated beaches. There are a total of 16 camping sites on the island that are open between April and October.

RESPONSIBLE TRAVEL

It doesn't take a lot to be environmentally friendly whilst travelling. Don't just think about your carbon footprint whilst flying to and from your holiday destination but also about how you can protect nature and culture abroad. As a tourist it is especially important to respect nature, look out for local products, cycle instead of driving, save water and much more. If you would like to find out more about eco-tourism please visit: www.ecotourism.org

From arrival to weather

Holiday from start to finish: the most important addresses and information for your trip to Crete

CAR HIRE

Cars from compact cars to jeeps, mopeds and motorbikes can be rented in all, bikes and mountain bikes in most of the holiday resorts on Crete. To rent a car you must have had your driver's license for more than a year and be over 21. A small car will cost from about 30 euros per day including miles driven, full comprehensive cover and tax.

CLIMATE & WHEN TO GO

Crete is not really a winter holiday destination. Between November and March it can rain and be quite cool. The best holiday months are from April to October. Swimming in the sea is best between May and November. May is the most beautiful time to travel in Crete, it is very green and there are flowers in bloom everywhere. It hardly rains from June to September; temperatures can reach 40 °C/104 °F) and the average temperatures for July and August are 30 °C/86 °F by day and 20 °C/68 °F at night. There are also often strong winds on Crete that can even bring the ferries to a standstill for hours in the summer.

CONSULATES & EMBASSIES

BRITISH VICE CONSULATE CRETE
Candia Tower | 17 Thalita Street | Ag. Dimitrios Sq. | Iráklio | tel. 28 10 22 40 12 | crete@fco.gov.uk

EMBASSY OF CANADA TO GREECE
48 Ethnikis Antistaseos Street | 15231 Chalandri | tel. 21 07 27 34 00 | www.canada international.gc.ca/greece-grece

EMBASSY OF THE UNITED KINGDOM
1 Ploutarchou Str. | 10675 Athens | tel. 21 07 27 26 00 | ukingreece.fco.gov.uk

U.S. EMBASSY
91 Vasilissis Sophias Avenue | 10160 Athens | tel. 21 07 21 29 51 | gr.usembassy.gov

CUSTOMS

EU citizens can import and export goods for their personal use tax-free (but only 800 cigarettes, 90 l of wine, 10 l of spirits). Visitors from other countries must observe the following limits, except for items for personal use. Duty free are: max. 50 g perfume, 250 cigarettes, 50 cigars, 250 g tobacco, 1 l of spirits (over 22 % vol.), 2 l of spirits (under 22 % vol.), 25 l of any wine. Gifts to the value of up to 175 euros may be brought into Greece.

DRINKING WATER

You can drink the (chlorinated) tap water everywhere except Iráklio. Still mineral water (metallikó neró) is also available in restaurants and cafés and is usually the same price as in the supermarkets.

DRIVING

When travelling to Crete with your own car, we recommend taking out a green insurance card even though it is not obligatory. The national driving license is also accepted in Greece. The maximum speed in towns is 50 km/h/31 mph and on national roads 90 km/h/56 mph. Maximum blood alcohol level is 0.5. Cretans are notorious for cutting curves, so always keep to the right of the road.

Also get used to honking at blind corners! During autumn, the roads are especially wet and slippery and care should be taken. Breakdown assistance can be obtained from the automobile club ELPA, country wide tel. 1 04 00.

EARTHQUAKES

Light earthquakes do occur every once in a while and are no reason to panic. Should you experience an earthquake you should take cover underneath a door frame, a table or a bed. As soon as the quake is over you should go outside (but do not use the lifts) and then stay clear of walls and flower pots that might topple over. Once outside follow the lead of the locals.

CURRENCY CONVERTER

£	€	€	£
1	1.15	1	0.88
3	3.45	3	2.64
5	5.75	5	4.40
13	14.95	13	11.44
40	46	40	35.20
75	86.25	75	66
120	138	120	105.60
250	287.50	250	220
500	575	500	440

$	€	€	$
1	0.90	1	1.10
3	2.70	3	3.30
5	4.50	5	5.50
13	11.70	13	14.30
40	36	40	44
75	67.50	75	82.50
120	108	120	132
250	225	250	275
500	450	500	550

For current exchange rates see www.xe.com

ELECTRICITY

Crete has the same 220 volt as most continental European countries. You will need an adapter if you want to use a UK plug.

EMERGENCY SERVICES

112 for all emergency services: police, fire brigade and ambulance. The number is toll free countrywide, English is spoken.

ENTRANCE FEES

Entry to all archaeological sites and state museums is free for children and youths, as well as students from EU member states who have appropriate ID. Senior citizens from EU countries 65 years and older get a 30 per cent discount.

HEALTH

Well-trained doctors guarantee basic medical care throughout Crete, however there is often a lack of technical equipment. If you are seriously ill, it is advisable to return home; this will be covered by your travel insurance. Emergency treatment in hospitals is free of charge and you can be treated for free by doctors if you present the European Health Insurance Card issued by your own insurance company. However, in practice doctors do so reluctantly and it is better to pay cash, get a receipt and then present your bills to the insurance company for a refund.

Most towns and villages have chemists that are are well-stocked but they may not always have British medication.

IMMIGRATION

A valid passport is required for entry into Greece. Children under 12 years need their own passport.

INFORMATION

The Hellenic Ministry of Culture and Tourism website provides explanations, photos and information on opening times and entrance prices of all excavations and many museums. Have a look at: *www.culture.gr*

GREEK NATIONAL TOURISM ORGANIZATION (UK)
4 Great Portland Street | London, W1W 8QJ | tel. 020 74 95 93 00 | www.visit greece.gr

GREEK NATIONAL TOURISM ORGANIZATION (US & CANADA)
800 3rd Avenue, 23rd floor | New York 10022 | tel. 212 4 21 57 77 | www.greek tourism.com

LANGUAGE

The Greeks are very proud of their language characters which are unique to Greece. More and more place names are being written in Roman letters as well but it is still helpful to have some knowledge of the Greek alphabet. However there is no uniform transliteration, so don't be surprised if you can encounter a place name in four different versions while you're there.

Sometimes the correct accents on addresses, hotel names and restaurant names are missing in this guide. The locals don't know them anyway; they seldom call places by their proper names. Cretans are used to name hotels and tavernas according to the owner's name and when giving addresses would rather name important points than a street name. Besides, the names of hotels and tavernas are not transliterated as they are pronounced, but rather the way they are written on signs.

BUDGETING

Boat tour	17.50–26.50 £/ 22.50–33.50 $ *all day, without transfer*
Coffee	1.30–2.65 £/ 1.70–3.35 $ *for an espresso*
Gyros	2–2.50 £/2.60–3.10 $ *for gyros and a pita bread*
Wine	2.20–5.30 £/ 2.80–6.70 $ *for a glass*
Petrol	1.55 £/1.95 $ *for a litre Super*
Deckchair	5.30–8.80 £/ 6.70–11.20 $ *per day together with umbrella*

NEWSPAPERS

English magazines and newspapers are available at most holiday resorts on the island. The weekly English Athens News is also published.

NUDIST BEACHES

Nude bathing is prohibited, but is practised on many isolated beaches. The only official nudist beach in Crete lies west of Chóra Sfakíon at the only nudist hotel in Greece, Hotel Vritomártis. Topless sunbathing is accepted everywhere.

OPENING HOURS

As a result of the economic crisis, the opening times of some museums and archaeological sites inland vary greatly. The number of attendants also drops significantly in autumn. Whether more staff will be recruited for the next season depends on the country's financial situation.

ORGANISED TOURS

All holiday resorts and hotels offer organised excursions by bus or boat. Bus tours are usually accompanied by local and licensed guides. Sometimes hikes and boat trips with transfer from the hotel to the harbour and back are on the programme.

PHONE & MOBILE PHONE

With the exception of some emergency numbers, all Greek telephone numbers have ten digits. There is no area dialling code. Greek mobile phone numbers always begin with "6". Telephone booths with card telephones are very common in the cities, villages and on country roads. They are mainly operated by the telephone company OTE/COSMOTE, which has offices in most cities. Telephone cards can also be bought at kiosks and supermarkets.

Reception for mobile phones is very good. When buying a Greek SIM card to obtain a Greek telephone number, you will always have to present identification. SIM cards can be bought from about 5 euros and remain valid for a year after last use. Mobile phone service providers are, among others, COSMOTE, Vodafone and WIND.

The dialling code for Greece is *0030* followed by the full ten digit telephone number. International dialling codes:

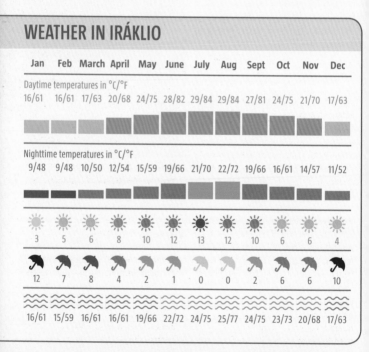

WEATHER IN IRÁKLIO

	Jan	Feb	March	April	May	June	July	Aug	Sept	Oct	Nov	Dec
Daytime temperatures in °C/°F												
	16/61	16/61	17/63	20/68	24/75	28/82	29/84	29/84	27/81	24/75	21/70	17/63
Nighttime temperatures in °C/°F												
	9/48	9/48	10/50	12/54	15/59	19/66	21/70	22/72	19/66	16/61	14/57	11/52
☀	3	5	6	8	10	12	13	12	10	6	6	4
☂	12	7	8	4	2	1	0	0	2	6	6	10
〜	16/61	15/59	16/61	16/61	19/66	22/72	24/75	25/77	24/75	23/73	20/68	17/63

United Kingdom *0044*, Australia *0061*, Canada *001*, Ireland *00353*, USA *001* followed by the area code without the zero.

POST

There are post offices in all cities and larger villages, open Mon–Fri 7am–3pm, in the tourism centres sometimes later in the afternoon as well as Saturday mornings.

TAXI

Taxis can be found everywhere and are relatively cheap. In the country they are called agoraíon and have no taxi meters – the price is calculated according to the distance.

TIME ZONE

Greece is two hours ahead of Greenwich Mean Time, seven hours ahead of US Eastern Time and seven hours behind Australian Eastern Time.

TIPPING

Tips are only expected in very touristy places. Greeks tend to give too much sometimes rather than always too little; small tips under 50 cents are seen as an insult. Tips are left on the table when leaving.

TOILETS

Apart from those in hotels, Crete's toilets can come as a surprise. They can be very posh and equipped with the latest Italian sanitary installations but at other times should only be used in emergencies. Be aware that even in the good hotels you are not allowed to flush the used toilet paper down the drain, but

Ottoman heritage – wooden balconies in the old town

have to throw it in the bin provided. The reason for this is that the paper clogs up the island's narrow sewers and soakaways.

YOUTH HOSTELS

In Crete there are several simple accommodation units calling themselves "youth hostels" but none of them is a member of the international Youth Hostel Association. They are mostly privately owned. The only "youth hostel" worth recommending is the one in Plakiás.

USEFUL PHRASES GREEK

PRONUNCIATION

We have provided a simple pronunciation aid for the Greek words
(see middle column). Note the following:

'   the following syllable is emphasised

ð   in Greek (shown as "dh" in middle column) is like "th" in "there"

θ   in Greek (shown as "th" in middle column) is like "th" in "think"

X   in Greek (shown as "ch" in middle column) is like a rough "h" or "ch" in
Scottish "loch"

Α	α	a	Η	η	i	Ν	ν	n	Τ τ t
Β	β	v, w	Θ	θ	th	Ξ	ξ	ks, x	Υ υ i, y
Γ	γ	g, i	Ι	ι	i, j	Ο	ο	o	Φ φ f
Δ	δ	d	Κ	κ	k	Π	π	p	Χ χ ch
Ε	ε	e	Λ	λ	l	Ρ	ρ	r	Ψ ψ ps
Ζ	ζ	s, z	Μ	μ	m	Σ	σ, ς	s, ss	Ω ώ o

IN BRIEF

Yes/No/Maybe	ne/'ochi/'issos	ναι/όχι/ίσως
Please/Thank you	paraka'lo/efcharis'to	παρακαλώ/ευχαριστώ
Sorry	sig'nomi	Συγνώμη!
Excuse me	me sig'chorite	Με συγχωρείτε!
May I...?	epi'treppete...?	Επιτρέπεται ...?
Pardon?	o'riste?	Ορίστε?
I would like to.../	,thelo.../	Θέλω .../
have you got...?	'echete...?	Έχετε ...?
How much is...?	'posso 'kani...?	Πόσο κάνει ...?
I (don't) like this	Af'to (dhen) mu a'ressi	Αυτό (δεν) μου αρέσει.
good/bad	ka'llo/kak'ko	καλό/κακό
too much/much/little	'para pol'li/pol'li/'ligo	πάρα πολύ/πολύ/λίγο
everything/nothing	ólla/'tipottal	όλα/τίποτα
Help!/Attention!/	vo'ithia!/prosso'chi!/	Βοήθεια!/Προσοχή!/
Caution!	prosso'chi!	Προσοχή!
ambulance	astheno'forro	Ασθενοφόρο
police/	astino'mia/	Αστυνομία/
fire brigade	pirosvesti'ki	Πυροσβεστική
ban/	apa'gorefsi/	Απαγόρευση/
forbidden	apago'revete	απαγορεύεται
danger/dangerous	'kindinoss/epi'kindinoss	Κίνδυνος/επικίνδυνος

Milás elliniká?

"Do you speak Greek?" This guide will help you to say the basic words and phrases in Greek.

GREETINGS, FAREWELL

Good morning!/after- noon!/evening!/night!	kalli'mera/kalli'mera!/ kalli'spera!/kalli'nichta!	Καλημέρα/Καλημέρα!/ Καλησπέρα!/Καληνύχτα!
Hello!/ goodbye!	'ya (su/sass)!/a'dio!/	Γεία (σου/σας)!/Αντίο!/
Bye!	ya (su/sass)!	Γεία (σου/σας)!
My name is...	me 'lene...	Με λένε …
What is your name?	poss sass 'lene?	Πως σας λένε?

DATE & TIME

Monday/Tuesday	dhef'tera/'triti	Δευτέρα/Τρίτη
Wednesday/Thursday	tet'tarti/'pempti	Τετάρτη/Πέμπτη
Friday/Saturday	paraske'vi/'savatto	Παρασκευή/Σάββατο
Sunday/weekday	kiria'ki/er'gassimi	Κυριακή/Εργάσιμη
today/tomorrow/yesterday	'simera/'avrio/chtess	Σήμερα/Αύριο/Χτες
What time is it?	ti 'ora 'ine?	Τι ώρα είναι?

TRAVEL

open/closed	annik'ta/klis'to	ανοικτό/κλειστό
entrance/ driveway	'issodhos/'issodhos ochi'matonn	Είσοδος/ Είσοδος οχημάτων
exit/exit (vehicles)	'eksodhos/ 'Eksodos ochi'matonn	Έξοδος/ Έξοδος οχημάτων
departure/ arrival	anna'chorissi/ 'afiksi	Αναχώρηση/ Αναχώρηση/Άφιξη
toilets/restrooms / ladies/ gentlemen	tual'lettes/gine'konn/ an'dronn	Τουαλέτες/Γυναικών/ Ανδρών
(no) drinking water	(óchi) 'possimo ne'ro	(όχι) Πόσιμο νερό
Where is...?/Where are...?	pu 'ine...?/pu 'ine...?	Πού είναι/Πού είναι …?
bus/taxi	leofo'rio/tak'si	Λεωφορείο/Ταξί
street map/ map	'chartis tis 'pollis/ 'chartis	Χάρτης της πόλης/ Χάρτης
harbour	li'mani	Λιμάνι
airport	a-ero'drommio	Αεροδρόμιο
schedule/ticket	drommo'logio/issi'tirio	Δρομολόγιο/Εισιτήριο
I would like to rent...	'thelo na nik'yasso...	Θέλω να νοικιάσω …
a car/a bicycle/a boat	'enna afto'kinito/'enna po'dhilato/'mia 'varka	ένα αυτοκίνητο/ένα ποδήλατο/μία βάρκα
petrol/gas station	venzi'nadiko	Βενζινάδικο
petrol/gas/diesel	ven'zini/'diesel	Βενζίνη/Ντίζελ

FOOD & DRINK

Could you please book a table for tonight for four?	Klis'te mass parakal'lo 'enna tra'pezi ya a'popse ya 'tessera 'atoma	Κλείστε μας παρακαλώ ένα τραπέζι γιά απόψε γιά τέσσερα άτομα.
The menu, please	tonn ka'taloggo parakal'lo	Τον κατάλογο παρακαλώ.
Could I please have...?	tha 'ithella na 'echo...?	Θα ήθελα να έχο ...?
with/without ice/ sparkling	me/cho'ris 'pago/ anthrakik'ko	με/χωρίς πάγο/ ανθρακικό
vegetarian/allergy	chorto'fagos/allerg'ia	Χορτοφάγος/Αλλεργία
May I have the bill, please?	'thel'lo na pli'rosso parakal'lo	Θέλω να πληρώσω παρακαλώ.

SHOPPING

Where can I find...?	pu tha vro...?	Που θα βρω ...?
pharmacy/ chemist	farma'kio/ ka'tastima	Φαρμακείο/Κατάστημα καλλυντικών
bakery/market	'furnos/ago'ra	Φούρνος/Αγορά
grocery	pandopo'lio	Παντοπωλείο
kiosk	pe'riptero	Περίπτερο
expensive/cheap/price	akri'vos/fti'nos/ti'mi	ακριβός/φτηνός/Τιμή
more/less	pio/li'gotere	πιό/λιγότερο

ACCOMMODATION

I have booked a room	'kratissa 'enna do'matio	Κράτησα ένα δωμάτιο.
Do you have any... left?	'echete a'komma...	Έχετε ακόμα ...?
single room	mon'noklino	Μονόκλινο
double room	'diklino	Δίκλινο
key	kli'dhi	Κλειδί
room card	ilektronni'ko kli'dhi	Ηλεκτρονικό κλειδί

HEALTH

doctor/dentist/ paediatrician	ya'tros/odhondoya'tros/ pe'dhiatros	Ιατρός/Οδοντογιατρός/ Παιδίατρος
hospital/emergency clinic	nossoko'mio/yatri'ko 'kentro	Νοσοκομείο/ Ιατρικό κέντρο
fever/pain	piret'tos/'ponnos	Πυρετός/Πόνος
diarrhoea/nausea	dhi'arria/ana'gula	Διάρροια/Αναγούλα
sunburn	ilia'ko 'engavma	Ηλιακό έγκαυμα
inflamed/injured	molli'menno/pligo'menno	μολυμένο/πληγωμένο
pain reliever/tablet	paf'siponna/'chapi	Παυσίπονο/Χάπι

POST, TELECOMMUNICATIONS & MEDIA

stamp/letter	gramma'tossimo/'gramma	Γραμματόσημο/Γράμμα
postcard	kartpos'tall	Καρτ-ποστάλ
I need a landline phone card	kri'azomme 'mia tile'karta ya dhi'mossio tilefoni'ko 'thalamo	Χρειάζομαι μία τηλεκάρτα για δημόσιο τηλεφωνικό θάλαμο.
I'm looking for a prepaid card for my mobile	tha 'ithella 'mia 'karta ya to kinni'to mu	Θα ήθελα μία κάρτα για το κινητό μου.
Where can I find internet access?	pu bor'ro na vro 'prosvassi sto índernett?	Που μπορώ να βρω πρόσβαση στο ίντερνετ?
socket/adapter/charger	'briza/an'dapporras/fortis'tis	πρίζα/αντάπτορας/φορτιστής
computer/battery/rechargeable battery	ippologis'tis/batta'ria/eppanaforti'zomenni batta'ria	Υπολογιστής/μπαταρία/επαναφορτιζόμενη μπαταρία
internet connection/wifi	'sindhessi se as'sirmato 'dhitio/vaifai	Σύνδεση σε ασύρματο δίκτυο/WiFi

LEISURE, SPORTS & BEACH

beach	para'lia	Παραλία
sunshade/lounger	om'brella/ksap'plostra	Ομπρέλα/Ξαπλώστρα

NUMBERS

0	mi'dhen	μηδέν
1	'enna	ένα
2	'dhio	δύο
3	'tria	τρία
4	'tessera	τέσσερα
5	'pende	πέντε
6	'eksi	έξι
7	ef'ta	εφτά
8	och'to	οχτώ
9	e'nea	εννέα
10	'dhekka	δέκα
11	'endhekka	ένδεκα
12	'dodhekka	δώδεκα
20	'ikossi	είκοσι
50	pen'inda	πενήντα
100	eka'to	εκατό
200	dhia'kossia	διακόσια
1000	'chilia	χίλια
10,000	'dhekka chil'iades	δέκα χιλιάδες

ROAD ATLAS

The green line indicates the Discovery Tour "Crete at a glance"
The blue line indicates the other Discovery Tours

All tours are also marked on the pull-out map

Photo: Shepherds on the Omalós high plain

Exploring Crete

The map on the back cover shows how
the area has been sub-divided

D   E   F   1

5 km
3.1 mi

Kólpos Chaníon

Stavrós Beach

Akrotíri

Ormos Koúni Limáni

Akr. Tríplii

Vardiés

Moní Katho

Spíleo A

Stavrós
Σταυρός 340 m

Moní Gou

Akr. Mavromoúri

418 m

Tersánas

Macherída Beach

Ormos Tersánas
Ormos Kaláthas

Chorafákia

Moní Agía T

Chordáki

Kalórrouma

Tavronítis Beach

Nisí
Ágii Theodóri
169 m

Ágios Onúfrios

Kaláthas

Kambáni

Mouz

Mále Beach

Platanias Beach

Chaniá Beach

Aptéra Beach

Eot Beach

Óasis Beach

Glaros Beach

Kounoupidianá

Koumbeli

Kounoupidianá

Moní Kathaniá

Péxares

Aetosel

Chaniá

Tavronítis

Máleme
Μάλεμε

Plataniás
Πλατανιάς

Marína

Kató
Stalós

Táfos Venizélos

Korakiés

Aróni

Arténemú

Platamítis

Géráni

Neá Kydonía

Pithári

Móro

Kipárissos

Modéa
Μοδέα

Stalós

Vamvakó
poula

**CHANIÁ
XANIA**

NAMFÍ Base

Sté
Στέ

Vríses
Loutráki
Psathogiánnos

**Ágios
Kir-Ioánnis**

Galatás

Óasi

Periváli
Περιβόλια

Mourniés
Μουρνιές

Soúda

NAMFÍ
Beach

M

Kerokámbi

Kirtomádos

Episkopí

Varípetro

Moní
Chrisopigís

Nerokoúros
Νεροκούρος

Tsikalariá

Akr. Soúd

Izzedi

oliópoulo

Koufós
Apothíkes

Agía

Aléfkanos
Αλικιανός

Témbla
542 m

Vandés

Farángi Georgitiko

Maláxa

Megáli
Chorafiá

Aptéra

merianá

Skonízo

Vatólakkos
Βατόλακκος

Fournés
Φουρνές

Panagía

Kontópoula

Farángi

Fárángi

Serviótissa

Derés

Skinés
Σκινές

Chliaró

Loúlos

Gerolákkos

Aletrouváni

Katóchori

Farángi Díktamos

Stílos

Néo Chori
Νέο Χωρι

Papadianá
Langós

Kásos

Orthoúni

Karés

Farángi Therisanó

Platívola

Drakóna

Kámbi

Mesklá
Μεσκλά

Thériso

Spíliaria

Simónas

Prówarma

Machéri

Paidochóri

Chostí

Kárános

Rizínia

Sotirós Christoú

Chalássi
1221 m

Ramni

Pemonia

Lákki

Mádaro

Karés

Melidóni

Frés
Φρές

Nípo

ímata

Xirokefália
1238 m

Zoúrva

Xerokokefála
1238 m

Kat. Vólíka
(EOS Chaniá)
1450 m

Tzitzifés

Prasés

Skidlá

NOMÓS CHANIÁ

Vat

1317 m

Nerantzóporta
1087 m

Katóros

Mávri
2069 m

Pírgos
571 m

Emb

Tourlí
1458 m

Kat. Kallérgi
(EOS Chaniá)
1677 m

1925 m

Línes
2093 m

Ágios Pnévma
2254 m

Vatoudi

Psári
1818 m

Melindaoú

**Ethnikós Drimós
Samariás**

Kat. Talkis
Koutsopoulos

Griás Sorós
2331 m

E4

Farángi Agía Iríni

Xilóskalo
1227 m

Ágios Nikólaos

Samariá

2347 m

Páchnes

Agriok+aía

1478 m

Kástro
2218 m

Ammoú

Psiláfi
1985 m

Gingilos
2080 m

Farángi Samariá

2452 m

Kakovóli
2214 m

Kat. Távri
(EOS Chaniá)
1240 m

Koustogérako

Volakías
2117 m

Psíritra
1795 m

Zaranokefála
2140 m

Trocharis
2401 m 2008 m

2243 m

Farángi Tripití

1315 m

Pálea
Agía Rouméli

Farángi Eligiás

Lefká Óri

Chalá

Ímbro

Tripití

Pikilássos

Tarrá

Agía Rouméli
Αγία Ρουμέλη

Ágios Ioánnis

Arádena
Αράδαινα

846 m

Anópolis

Farángi Ímbro

Farángi Arádena

Livanianá

**Ágios
Pávlos**

Chóra Sfakíon
Χώρα Σφακίων

Akr. Kalótrίdíos

Domáta Beach

Ormos
Agía Rouméli

Finíkas

Loutró

Finí

Ormos Finíka

143

Ormos Finíka

Stavrós Beach

Akrotíri

Vardiés
340 m

Moní Katholikó
Spíleo Arkoudiótissa
Akr. Maléka

Akr. Trip.

Stávros Σταυρός
Akr. Mavromoúri

418 m

Moní Gouvernéto

Macherída Beach
Órmos Tersánas

Koumarés
Tersánas
Chorafákia

Moní Agía Triáda

Sklópa
528 m

Seïtán Limánia Beach

Órmos Kaláthas

Ágios Onúfrios
Kounoupidianá
Koumbéli

Kalathás

Kalórrouma

Mouzourás

Perivólitsa
Akr. Toúrkak.

Tálos Venizélos

Korakiés

Moní
Kalegréon
Paxinós

Kambáni

Aeradrómio
Chaniá

Vígles
195 m

Akr. Pelegrí

Piraíus

CHANIÁ
XANIÁ

Pitbári
Aróni

Anemóni

Stérnes
Στέρνες

Maráthi

Nisí
Paleosoúda

NAMFI Base
94

NAMFI
Beach

Minoá

Nisí Soúda

A 90

Soúda
Tsikaloú

Órmos Souda

Akr. Drápano
87 m

Nerokoúros
Νερoκoύρος

E 75

Megáli
Chorafiá

Kalámi
Izzedín

Akr. Souda

Kalíves
Beach

Órmos
Vaskoú

Malákisopigis
Vandés

610 m

Kontópoula

Aptéra

Pláka

Kókkino Chorió
Καλυβές

Akr. Schoinés

letrouvári
Loúlos
Gerolákkos

Katochóri

Farángi Georgítiko

Farángi

Farángi Díktamos

Serviótissa
Stílos

Almiridá
Tsiváras

Doulianá
Aspro

Kambiá Drapanokéfala
527 m

Gavalochóri
Palelóni

Ombrósgialos
Akr. Konismátsa

Kefalás Κεφαλάς

erisianó

Platívola
Kámbi
Samónas

Próvarma

Arméni

Néo Chorió
Néo Χωριό

Vámos
Βάμος

Xirostérni

Órmos

akóna
Spiliária

Machéri

Agii Pándes

Litsárda

kéfala

Christoú
Chalássi
1221 m

Mádaro

Ramni
Karés

Paidochóri

Pemónia

Melidóni

Frés
Φρές

Nípos

Kalamítsi
Alexándrou

Sellía
Likotinaréa

Kalamítsi
Amigdáli

Georgioúpoli
Γεωργιούπολη

Kaliváki Beach

Georgioúpoli Beach

Kat. Vólika
(EOS Chaniá)
1450 m

Tzitzifés

Vafés

Vríses
Βρύσες

Exópoli

Kavrós

E 75

Pírgos
571 m

Máza

Fonés

Aspoulliani

Drám.

Lines
2093 m

Mávri
2069 m

Ágios Pnévma
2254 m

Embrósneros

Alíkambos

Mathés

Limni
Kournás

Moúri
Kávallos

Episkop.
Επισκoπ.

Vatoudiáris

Griás Sorós
2331 m

Chalára
1068 m

Kournás
Κουρνάς

Kastéll

Kat. Talkis
atsopoulos

E4

Agriokéfala

Xilódema
800 m

Karés

Farángi Katré

Tripáli
1494 m

Pátima

2347

Páchnes
2452 m

Kástro
2218 m

Ammoúdari
Petres

Kástro Othomanikó

Omanite
1158 m

Argiroúpo
Αργυρούπο

iá

Trocharis
2214 m

Kakovóli

Kat. Távri
(EOS Chaniá)
1240 m

Goní

Asígonia
Ασήγωνια

Marouloú

2401 m 2008 m

ranokéfala
2140 m 2243 m

Méga Órós
1181 m

Angathés

Agriokéfala
1074 m

Arolit.

Lefká Óri

Chalára
Ímbros

Akónes

Kallikrátis

Miriokéfala
Ro

Sfa

1046 m

Ágios Ioánnis

Arádena
Αράδαινα

846 m

Farángi Ásfendou

Perisináki
1085 m

Farángi
Kallikrátiano

Katapóri

Krion
1228 m 131

Farángi Arádena

Livianiá

Farángi Ímbros

Komitádes

Asfendos
1083 m

1043 m

Áno
Rodákino

Mor
Káτ

Finikas
Fínix

Chóra Sfakíon
Χώρα Σφακίων

Nomikianá

Patsianós
Kapsodásos

Skaloti

Argoulés

Roc

Loutró

Ágios
Nektários

Frango-
kástelo

Kóraka

Órmos Finikiá

Mbanara Beach

Lýkos Beach

Akr. A. Kirikí

Frýdni Beach

Koutelós Beach

Frangokástello

Lákki Beach

Polyrízos Beach

Kórakas Beach

Ílingas Beach

Glíka Nerá Beach

Frangokástello

Akr. Frangokástello

Katonisi

Órthi Ámmos Beach

Agía Marína Beach

Gávdos

Livikó Pélagos

144

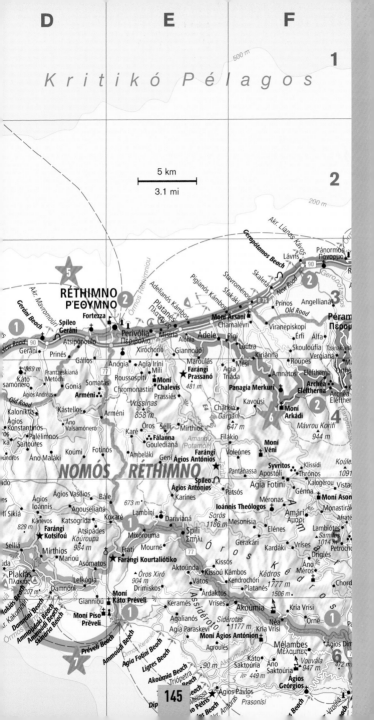

D   **E**   **F**

1

Kritikó Pélagos

500 m

2

5 km
3.1 mi

200 m

Ormós Rethímnou

Akr. Liános Kávos

Geropótamos Beach

Pánormos
Πάνορμος

Lávris

Skaletá

2

Gero potamos

New Road

90

Prinos
Old Road

Angelliana

3

5

RÉTHIMNO
PEΘYMNO

2

Fortezza

Adelianós Kámbos

Stavroménos

Sfakáki

E 75

Moní Arsáni

Viranepiskopí

Pérama
Πέραμα

Akr. Mavronoúri

Gerání Beach

1

Spíleo
Gerání

Atsipópoulo

Perivólia
Πλατανές
Misiría

Adele

Pigi

Loútra

Erfi
Alfa

Skouloúfia
Vergianá

Tzanakáki

2

New Road

90

Gerání

Prinés

Gálios

Anógia

Agía Iríni

Mili

Maroulás

Mési

Kiriánna

Roupes

Eléftherna

Archéa
Eléftherna

Xirochóri

Giannoudi

Agía Triáda

Amnatos

Orthé

4

Káto
samonéro

Agios Andréas

Frantzeskianá
Metóchi

Goniá

Somatás

Roussospíti

Chromonastíri

Farángi
Prassanó

Panagía Merkúri

Kavoúsi

Moní
Arkádi

2

Archéa
Eléftherna

Old Road

Kaloníkris
Agios
Konstantínos

Ano
Valsamónero

Kástelos

Arméni

Moní
Chalévis

481 m

Vrissinás
858 m

Chárkia

Gargáni
647 m

Mávrou Korifí
944 m

Saitoúres

Koúmi

Ano Malaki

Karé

Óros Sélli

Mirthios

Filákio

Moní
Véni

NOMÓS RÉTHIMNO

Fotinós

Fálanna
Gouledianá

Ambeláki

Geni Ágios Antónios

Voleónes

Pantánassa

Syvritos
Apostóli

Klissídi
Thrónos

Koúle
1091 m

1

Ágios Vasílios

Bále

673 m

Spíleo
Ágios Antónios

Karínes

Patsós

Agía Fotiní

Génna

Kalogérou

Moní Ason

Vistagi

Monastiráki

Ágios
Ioánnis

Agouselianá

Lambíni

Darivianá

Ioánnis Theólogos

Méronas

Amári
Amári

Lambiótes

Afratés

Samiles
1014 m

Kánevos

Katsográda

Mixórouma

Sorós
1186 m

Mesonísia

Elénes

Kardáki

Vríses

Drigiés

Petrochó

Farángi
Kotsifoú

Atsipádes

Koúroupa
984 m

Spíli
Σπήλι

Mourné

77

Gerakári

Ano
Méros

1

829 m

Selliá

Mirthios

Marioú

Asómatos

Farángi Kourtaliótiko

Frati

Óros Xiró
904 m

Kissós

Kissoú Kámbos

Vátos

Drimiskos

Aktoúnda

Kédros
1777 m

Platanés

1506 m

Chord

Plakiás
Πλακιάς

207 m

Lefkógia

Damnóni

Giannioú

Moní
Káto Préveli

Keramés

Vríses

Akoúmia

Kría Vrísi

Néa
Orne

1

Kría Vrísi

Sidérotas
1177 m

Moní Píso
Préveli

Agalianós

Agía Paraskeví

Moní Ágios Antónion

Kría Vrísi

Ágios Dim

7

Préveli Beach

Agía Fotiní Beach

Ligres Beach

Ammoúdi Beach

Agroúles

Káto
Saktoúria

Mélambes
Μέλαμπες

Vouvála
947 m

472 m

Ano
Saktoúria

6

Kakómouri

Dámnoni Beach

Ammoúdaki Beach

Ammoúdi Beach

Skinária Beach

Akoúmia Beach

Triópetra
Beach

90 m

449 m

Ágios
Geórgios

Ágios Dim

145

Melissa Beach

Ágios Pávlos

Ágios Pávlos
Beach

Dip Beach

Prasonísi

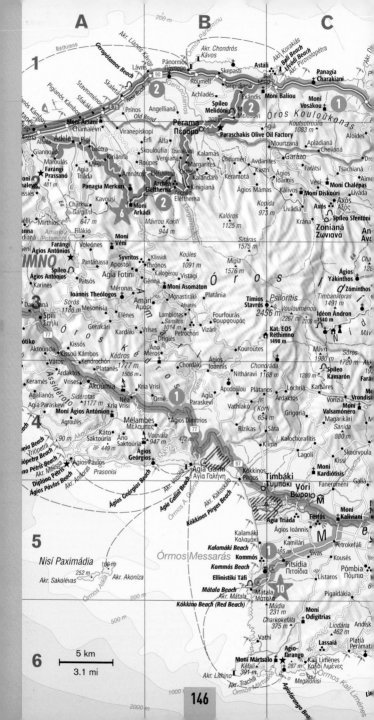

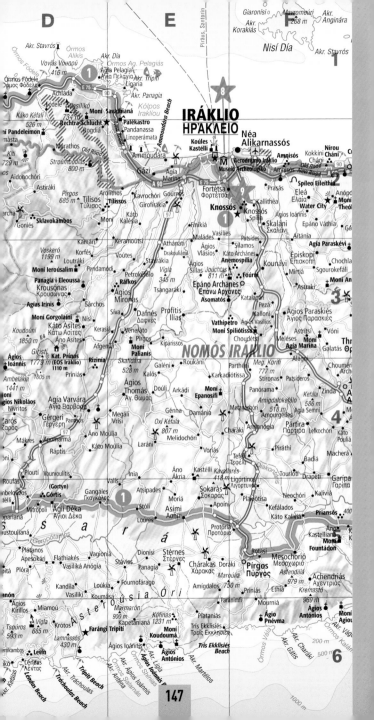

Giaronísi o
Nisí Petalidi
Mavromoúri
Akr. Marmara
Akr. Angínara
Akr. orakiás
268 m

B

Nisí Paximádi

1
Nisí Día
Akr. Stavrós

Néa Alikarnassós
Aerodrómio Iráklio
Archeologikó
99
Amnissós
Kokkíni Cháni
Chani
Amnisós
New Road
Old Road
Nírou
Cháni
A 90
90
Goúves
Agriáno
CretAquarium
Flíkas
Gournés
E 75
Analipsí
Anissáras
Anissáras Beach
Akr. Chersónisos
Liménas
Chersonísou
Λ. Χερσονήσου
92
Piskopianó
Lyttos Beach
Stalida Beach
Mália Beach
Eastern Pi

Prasás
Eleá
Ελαία
Spíleo Eileíthia
Anópoli
Spíleo Skotinó
Water City
Moní Theológou
Skotinó
Chersónisos
Χερσονήσου
Koutouloufári
Acquapark
Pirgiá
Stalida
Stalída
Σταλίδα
Mália
Mál
580 m
Vigla
534 m
4

Kallithéa
Knossós
Spília
Ágios Ioánnis
Skaláni
Σκαλάνι
Epáno Váthia
Vorítsi
Kóxari
Kaló Chorió
Charasó
Máza
480 m
Mochós
Móchos
Mália
Μάλια
801

Patsídes
ilamos
rchánes
ospília
Foúrni
Aïtánia
Agía Paraskeví
Gálipe
Galifa
Smári
Aféndis Christós
Lagós
Potamiès
Ποταμιές
Moní Gouverniótissa
Sfendíli
Ráchi
801 m

Katalágari
Pezá
Kallóni
Ágios Vasílios
Επίσκοπι
Epískopi
Chochlakiés
Sgourokefáli
Mirtiá
Astrakí
Kounávi
Pigí
Káto
Karouzaná
Avdoú
Αβδού
Gωνιές
Góniés
Kerá
Rozas Gorge
Moní Kerá
Kardiótissa
Ámbelos Afin
900 m
M
Hom

iótiss
houdétsi
Ágios Paraskiés
Αγιος Παρασκιές
Apóstoli
Απόστολοι
Sambás
Zofóri
Ágios
Pandeleímon
Littos
Aski
Louloudáki
1107 m
Pinakianó
Pinakiano
1

RAKLIO
Astrítsi
Véni
Meléses
Agia Marina
Moní
Galatás
Thrapsanó
Θραψανό
Evangelismós
Kastélli
Καστέλλι
Kastamonítsa
Xidás
Tíchos
Moní Vidianís
Káto Metóchi
11
Lassíthi
Kristall

Meg. Korifí
777 m
Alági
Choúmeri
Archontikó
Roussochória
Agía
Paraskeví
Amarianó
Lilianó
Máthia
Ágios Chárálambos
Pláti
Aféndis
1578 m
Psichró
Ψυχρό
Avre
kóno

Stíronas
Patsideró
Zinda
Kefála
586 m
Agia Semni
Mousoúta
Áno Poullá
Geráki
Γεράκι
Koprokefála
Nípiditos 984 m
Sarakinó
1588 m
Diktéo
Andro
Kamináki

Panórama
Amigdalokefáló
518 m
Pártira
Πάρτιρα
Lefkochóri
Káto
Poullá
Monashráki
Arkádes
Afráti
1462 m
Virgiméno
1414 m
Mageréftra
1462 m

Piráthi
Machera
Íni
Ίνιο
Kasános
Thomadianó
Émbaros
Xeniákos
Katofígi
Milliarádes
Aféndis Chri
2141 m

jórtino
jórtino
Tourlotí
Drapéti
Garípa
Γαρίπα
Karavádos
Mártha
Koupá
1187 m
Aplíki
1183 m
1341 m

Plakiótissa
Neochóri
Kefálados
Kalivía
Lagoúta
Skiniás
Σκινιάς
Mési
Loutráki
Káto
Viánnos
Áno Viánnos
Άνω Βιάννος
Amirás
Péfkos
Krewat
Ágios
Vasilic

Rotási
Kefálados
Káto Kalivía
Priansós
400 m
Áno
Kastelliana
Káto
Kastelliana
Demáti
Δεμάτι
Kefála Chóndrou
Farángi
Áno Viánnos
Vachós
Agía Moní
1
Faráng

Pírgos
Πύργος
Mesochório
Μεσοχώριο
Asfendiliá
Achendriás
Αχεντριάς
Kremastó
Inatos
Tsoútsouros
Τσούτσουρος
Dérmatos
Chóndros
735 m
Cháfsakas
632 m
Pezepés
Kastri
Keratókambos
Arvi
Αρβή
Moní
Arví
Faf

Primás
nfi
Mourniá
Ethiá
979 m
969 m
Ágios
Antónios
Moní
Agíou Nikíta
Ágio
Pnévma

148

D　**E**　**F**

Kritikó Pélagos

1

5 km
3.1 mi

2

Akr. Poúnta
Ormos Pópou

Paralía Milátou
Spíleo
Mílatos
Epáno Sísi
Anginarás
307 m

Moní Agía Andréa
Koudoúmalos
Amigdáles
Anógia
Kounáli
Nofaliás
Agía Andréa
Vlichádia
Finokaliá
KKáto Sélles
Mironikítas
Ágios Geórgios
Sélles
Vrouchás
Akr. Kástri
Akr. Ágios Ioánnis
Akr. Fátsi

Panagía Selinári
ni Ágios chasióti
Vrachási
Βραχάσι
Moní Xera Xíla
Stavrós
794 m
Perámbela
Dóries
Moní Aretíou
Áno Pinés
Karidí
Tsiflíki
Pláka
Πλάκα
Spinalónga
Nisí Kalidón
Nisí Spinalónga

Ládo
Latsída
Λατσίδα
Neápoli
Νεάπολη
Vouliśméni
Kastélli
Kouroúnes
Mavrikianó
Káto Pinés
Eloúnta
Ελούντα
Loútra
140 m
Oloús
Akr. Vángi
Nisí Kolokíthia
Kolokíthia Beach
Akr. Pórou

Séna Oros
Tsekoúra
998 m 915 m
Arkoláki
Dríros
Dilakos
Límnes
Λίμνες
Ágios Ioánnis
Choumeriákos
Dríkos
Lénika
Akr. Pleóra

Seléna
599 m
Museum
Macherá
1487 m
Éxo Potámi
Zénia
Anginarás
577 m
Kartérides
Adrianós
Xirókambos
Katsikiá
Chavánia Beach
Ágios Nikólaou
Akr. Pleóra
Nisí Ágios Pándes
Kólpos Mirambé
Nisí Psi

Iádo
Patéra tá Sélla
100 m
Mésa Lassíti
ios Konstantínos
eórgios Αγ. Γεώργιος
Amigdáli
Éxo Lakkonía
Flamourianá
Tápes
ÁGIOS NIKÓLAOS
ΑΓ. ΝΙΚΟΛΑΟΣ
Kitroplatía Beach
Almirós Beach
Ammoundára Beach

Katharó Tsiví
Farángi Krítsa (Kritsa-Schlucht)
1564 m
Vóina
Kritsá
Κριτσά
Lató
Thílakas
521 m
Panagía i Kerá
Mardáti
Vathí
Ammoundára
Kaló Chorió Beach
Ormos Chorioú
Voulísma Beach
Akr. Macharídi
Nisí Konída

Katharó
Ágios Ioánnis Théol.
Kroústa
Κρούστα
134 m
Ístro
Akr. Macharídi
Vrionísi

os
Lázaros
2085 m
Avdeliákos
Kourelí
1396 m
NOMÓS LASSÍTHI
Ágios Sílas
Pírgos
Vrókastro
Kaló Chorió
Καλό Χωριό
Gourniá
Pachiá Ámmos
Παχειά Άμμος

Ókri
Selákano
Mathokotsaná
Máles
Μάλες
Málé
1141 m
Prína
Meseléri
Moní Faneroménis
Skinávria Korifí
698 m
Óleros
Plakokefála
712 m
Stavrós
Papoúra
1011 m
Vasilíki
Farái

Christós
Metaxochóri
adára
783 m
Moní Pan. Exakoútis
Lárissa
Καλαμαύκα
Kalamáfka
Psathí
Ágios Geórgios
Makriliá
Papadianá
Episkopí
Ágios Ioán
Αγιος Ιωάνν
Kato Chorió
Κάτω Χωριό
Katalima
803 m
Monastiráki

Simí
Kaïménos
Ríza
Mithi
Mourniés
(Sarakiná-Schlucht)
Farángi Sarakiná
Kamára
Kéfala
312
Fragma
Bramianá
Anatolí
Ανατολή
Kalógen
Kendrí
Κεντρί
Vainiá
Koutsounári

Sikoúlogos
Loutráki
Gdóchia
Pýrgos Mýrtos
Foúrnou Koryfí
Ammoudáres
Néa
Anatolí
Stómio
Grá Ligiá
Γρά Λυγιά
Bramianá
Potámi
Ierápetra
Ιεράπετρα
Ierápetra Beach
Ormos Ierápetras
Akr. Ierápetra
Akr. Kater

sari
ráda
Tértsa
Mírtos
Μύρτος
Néa Mírtos
Mírtos Beach
Vátos
Akr. Xeromíli
Tértsa Beach
Akr. Theofílou
Ormos Tértsa
Néa
Anatolí
Kalamáki

Liviko Pélagos
Livikó
Pélagos

6

149

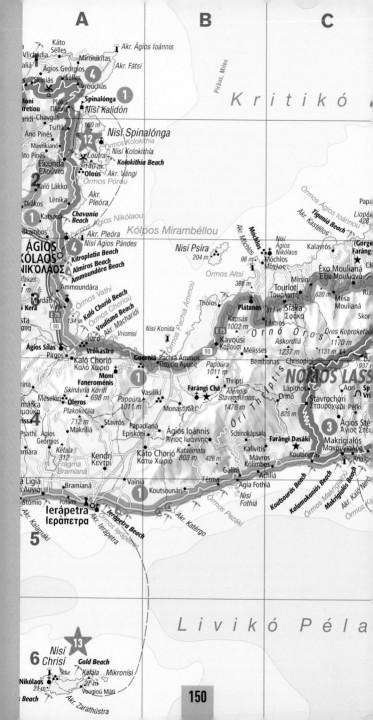

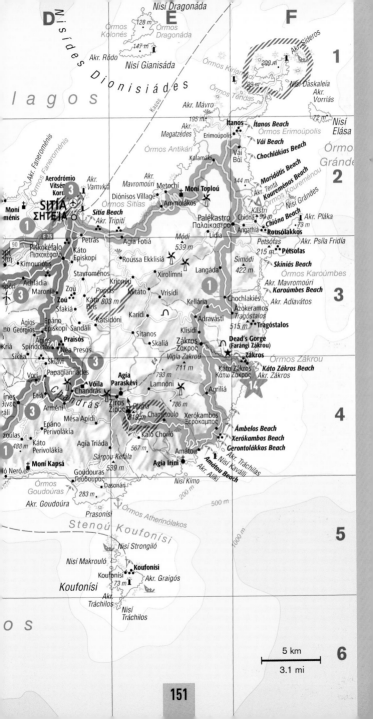

D

Nisídes Dionisiádes

Nisí Dragonáda

Órmos Kolonés
128 m.
Órmos Dragonáda

Akr. Ródo
147 m.

Nisí Gianisáda

E

F

Akr. Síderos
209 m.

Órmos Kiriamádi
199 m
Nisí Dáskaleía
Akr. Vorriás

Órmos Téndas

72 m
Nisí Elása

1

l a g o s

Akr. Faneroménis

Órmos Faneroménis

Akr. Mávro
195 m
Akr. Megatzédes
Ítanos
Erimoúpolis

Ítanos Beach
Órmos Erimoúpolis

Órmos Antikári
Kalamáki

Akr. Vamvíka

Akr. Mavromoúri

Aeródrómio Vítséi Korr.

Diónisos Village
Órmos Sitías

Moní Toploú

Metochí

Ammolákos

Vái Beach
Vái Bái

Chochlákias Beach

144 m

Maridátis Beach

Akr. Tentá
Koureménos Beach
Órmos Kouremenou

Nisí Grándes

Órmo Gránde

2

SITÍA ΣΗΤΕΙΑ

3

Moní ménis
1

Sitía Beach
Akr. Tripití

Petrás

Palékastro
Παλαίκαστρο
Lidía

Kástri
90 m
Chioná
Angathía

Chióna Beach
Akr. Pláka
73 m

Rousólakkos

Piskoképhalo
Πισκοκέφαλο
Kimouriótis

Káto Episkopí
Agia Fotiá

Módi
539 m

Petsófas
215 m

Pétsofas
Akr. Psíla Fridía

Roússa Ekklisiá
Stavroménos
Krionéri

Xirolímni

1

Langáda

Simódi
422 m

Skiniás Beach
Órmos Karoúmbes

Achládia
3
Maronía
Zoú
Pruás
Mitáto

Káto
Dris
Zoú
Sfakiá
Katsidóni

Kató 803 m Dris

Vrisídi
Karídi

Kelláría

Chochlakiés
Adravásti

Akr. Mavromoúri
Karoúmbes Beach
Akr. Adiavátos

Ázokeramos
Tragóstalos
515 m

Tragóstalos

3

Ágios Georgios
Kriá
Sikéa

Epáno Episkopí Sandáli
Sitanos

Praisós

Ágios Spiridónas
Néa Presós

Sklaví
Papagiánnades

3

Klisídi

Skaliá
Vigla Zakroú

Dead's Gorge (Farángi Zákrou)

Zákros
Ζάκρος

Zákros

Káto Zákros
Κάτω Ζάκρος
Káto Zákros

Káto Zákros Beach
Akr. Zákros

Órmos Zákrou

14

4

Chandrás

Etiá
Armení

Voíla
Chandrás

Agia Paraskévi

793 m
711 m

Lamnóni

Agriliá

3

Epáno Perivolákia
Mésa Apídi

Zíros
Ζίρος
Pugá
786 m

Chametoúlo

Xerókambos
Ξερόκαμπος

Ámbelos Beach

1
488 m
Káto Perivolákia

Agia Triáda

Moní Kapsá

Sárgou Kefála
589 m

Kaló Chorió
567 m

Amátou

Agia Iríni

Xerókambos Beach
Gerontolákkos Beach
Akr. Tráchilas

Amátou Beach

Nisí Kavállí
Akr. Aílki

819 m

Goúdouras
Γούδουρας
Dasáni

283 m

Nisí Kímo

Órmos Atherinólakos

500 m

Órmos Goudoúras

Akr. Goudoúra

Prasonísi

Stenoú Koufonísi

1000 m

5

Nisí Strongiló

Nisí Makroúlo

Koufonísi
73 m
Akr. Graigós

Koufonísi

Koufonísi

Akr. Tráchilos

Nisí Tráchilos

O S

5 km
3.1 mi

6

KEY TO ROAD ATLAS

Autobahn mit Nummer / Motorway with number	Burg; Burgruine / Castle; castle ruin
Schnellstraße / Clearway	Schloss / Palace
Fernstraße mit Nummer / Highway with number (90)	Kirche; Kirchenruine / Church; church ruin
Hauptstraße mit Nummer / Main road with number	Kloster; Klosterruine / Monastery; monastery ruin
Nebenstraßen / Secondary road	Denkmal / Monument
Straße ungeteert / Road unpaved	Turm / Tower
Straße in Bau; in Planung / Road under construction; projected	Leuchtturm / Lighthouse
Fahrweg / Carriage way	Windräder / Wind engines
Distriktgrenze / District border	Sendemast / Aerial mast
Sperrgebiet / Prohibited area	Sehenswürdigkeit / Point of interest
Nationalpark, Naturreservat / National park, nature reserve	Archäologische Stätte / Archeological site
Korallenriff / Coral reef	Berghütte / Mountain hut
Jugendherberge / Youth hostel	Berggipfel; Höhenpunkt / Mountain top; geodetic point
Jachthafen / Marina	Paß / Pass
Ankerplatz, Hafen / Anchorage, harbour	Höhle / Cavern
Schnorcheln / Skin diving	Aussichtspunkt / Panoramic view
Tauchen / Diving	Badestrand / Beach
Windsurfing / Windsurfing	Internationaler Flughafen / International airport
Wasserski / Water skiing	Flugplatz / Aerodrome

MARCO POLO Erlebnistour 1 / MARCO POLO Discovery Tour 1

MARCO POLO Erlebnistouren / MARCO POLO Discovery Tours

1 MARCO POLO Highlight

MARCO POLO TRAVEL GUIDES

The travel guides with
Insider
Tips

INDEX

This index lists all places mountains, lakes and islands plus several keywords featured in this guide. Numbers in bold indicate a main entry.

WRITE TO US

e-mail: info@marcopologuides.co.uk
Did you have a great holiday?
Is there something on your mind?
Whatever it is, let us know!
Whether you want to praise, alert us
to errors or give us a personal tip –
MARCO POLO would be pleased to
hear from you.
We do everything we can to provide the
very latest information for your trip.

Nevertheless, despite all of our authors'
thorough research, errors can creep in.
MARCO POLO does not accept any
liability for this. Please contact us by
e-mail or post.
MARCO POLO Travel Publishing Ltd
Pinewood, Chineham Business Park
Crockford Lane, Chineham
Basingstoke, Hampshire RG24 8AL
United Kingdom

PICTURE CREDITS
Cover photograph: Bay with fishing boat (Schapowalow/SIME: Johanna Huber)
Photos: Marios Chalkiadakis (18 top); DuMont Bildarchiv: T. Gerber (46/47), Modrow (135), Spitta (117); Getty-
ima...
(2, 7...
54/5...
68/6...
(56)...
Laif/...
Look...
(19 t...
113, ...
mau...
ima...
gou...
Pict...

3rd ...
Wor...
Croc...
© M...
Chie...
Auth...
Prog...
Tim ...
Wha...
Cartography road atlas: DuMont Reisekartografie, Fürstenfeldbruck; © MAIRDUMONT, Ostfildern
Cartography pull-out map: DuMont Reisekartografie, Fürstenfeldbruck; © MAIRDUMONT, Ostfildern
Cover design, p. 1, pull-out map cover: Karl Anders – Büro für Visual Stories, Hamburg; design inside:
milchhof:atelier, Berlin; p. 2/3, Discovery Tours: Susan Chaaban Dipl.-Des. (FH)
Translated from German by Wendy Barrow, Susan Jones, Jennifer Walcoff Neuheiser and Mo Croasdale
Editorial office: SAW Communications, Redaktionsbüro Dr. Sabine A. Werner, Mainz: Julia Gilcher, Cosima Talhouni,
Dr. Sabine A. Werner; prepress: SAW Communications, Mainz, in cooperation with
alles mit Medien, Mainz
Phrase book in cooperation with Ernst Klett Sprachen GmbH, Stuttgart,
Editorial by PONS Wörterbücher

MIX
Paper from
responsible sources
FSC® C124385

DOS & DON'TS 👆

Even in Crete, there are a few things you should bear in mind

DON'T UNDERESTIMATE THE DANGER OF FIRES

The risk of a forest fire on Crete is high. Smokers must be especially careful and should never discard their cigarette butts.

DO PARK LEGALLY

Parking illegally is very expensive: 80 euros is what this indulgence will cost you. Other traffic violations are also heavily fined.

DON'T BE SHOCKED BY THE PRICE OF FISH

Fresh fish is very expensive and is often sold by weight. Always ask for the kilo price first and when the fish is being weighed, make sure you are present to avoid any unpleasant surprises on the bill.

DO COVER UP IN THE CHURCHES

Cretans are used to seeing some skin in the beach resorts but in the villages, you should dress more conservatively. In the churches and monasteries it is expected that knees and shoulders be covered.

DON'T TAKE ARTEFACTS

On the beach and in the mountains no one will mind if you collect a pebble or two but taking a stone that has been crafted into something or ceramic shards from an archaeological site is a criminal offence.

DO PAY THE COVER CHARGE

Most restaurant bills have some incomprehensible entries: 0.25–2 euros per person cover charge. Theoretically this cost is for cutlery, bread and napkins. In practice, it is a general charge and even if you do not use any cutlery or eat any bread, you have to pay it.

DON'T PHOTOGRAPH WITHOUT PERMISSION

Many Cretans love to have their photograph taken, but dislike tourists that act as though they are on safari. Before you just start snapping away, smile at the person you want to photograph and wait for their permission.

DON'T PUT YOUR FOOT IN IT

Please do not ask for a serviette in English – they will not understand you. That's because the Greek word "serviettay" means something some ladies need for a few days every month. Sign language can also be quite tricky. A stretched index finger means "1", and a light shake of the head means "Yes"!

DO STAY ON THE TARMAC

If you are travelling with a hired vehicle and leave the main road, you will be driving without insurance and will have to pay for any damages yourself. That sometimes even goes for 4 × 4 vehicles! Tyre damage is not insured most of the time, even if the damage occurred on a tarmac road.